THE
BIBLE

IN THE ARMENIAN TRADITION

THE BIBLE

IN THE ARMENIAN TRADITION

Vrej Nersessian

THE BRITISH LIBRARY

First published in 2001 by
The British Library
96 Euston Road
London NW1 2DB

British Library Cataloguing in Publication data
A catalogue record for this title is available from
The British Library

ISBN 0 7123 4698 8

Designed by Andrew Shoolbred
Printed in Hong Kong by South Sea International Press

Contents

1 Portraits of the four Evangelists from the
Gospels by Melk'isedek, Berkri, north-eastern
shore of Lake Van, 1338.
Matenadaran, Erevan, ms. 4813, f.5v.

Foreword

In *The Bible in the Armenian Tradition* Dr Vrej Nersessian tells Western readers about the Armenian Bible's significance for the Armenian people. He also brings the work of some Armenian scholars to the attention of a wider audience.

The Armenian Bible, long admired for its elegance and accuracy, has been called 'the queen of translations'. It gives important insights to its Greek 'parent' as some ancient texts which have not survived in Greek have been preserved in Armenian translation. Two such are Philo's *Questions on Genesis*, and Books IV and V of Irenaeus of Lyon's *Against Heresies*. Some Bibles preserve hexaplaric signs and readings of Aquila, which do not survive anywhere else, thus being an important witness to Origen's epic work on the text of the Bible.

Dr Nersessian explains how the need for a written Bible led to the invention of the Armenian alphabet, which in turn sparked off the whole Armenian literature. He introduces us to Sahak and Mesrop, principally responsible for the translation of the Bible, and gives vivid quotations from the early historians Koriwn, Ghazar P'arpetsi and Movses Khorenatsi. We learn how having a Bible in their own language helped the Armenians preserve their sense of nationhood, torn as they were between Rome and Persia, the two superpowers of the day.

These days we are more conscious that the Bible is a living text, changing to suit the local needs of Christians. We should not be too surprised to find the Armenian Bible was not sure whether Revelation was to be accepted, but included some extra books, such as Paul's Third Letter to the Corinthians. But the greatest surprise is that so many Bibles have long colophons, which give details of the sponsor, the scribe and a good deal of other extremely valuable historical information.

We are accustomed in the West to a rather half-hearted defence of images, which are condescendingly described as 'books for the illiterate'. It is refreshing to read a full-blooded defence of images: for example, according to Nerses Shnorhali, the sensual pleasures of illuminated Bibles are not for simple folk, but rather for the initiate they are 'baths of sight and hearing for those approaching the soaring peaks of God'.

T. S. Pattie
Former Curator of The British Library's
Manuscript Collections
January 2001

Introduction

The Bible is the central book of Western civilization. It holds a unique and exclusive status, not merely in terms of the religious history of the Christian world, but also in literary history, and even in what might be called our collective cultural memory.

The English word 'bible' is derived, via French, from the late Latin *biblia*, a feminine singular noun that meant simply 'book'. In its older Latin form, however, *biblia* was not understood as the feminine singular, but as the neuter plural form, which was, in turn, derived from the Greek *ta biblia*, which meant 'the books' – essentially no more than a collection of individual works. This shift in meaning reflects the changing physical conditions of the books themselves. Before the invention of the large, multi-quire book, the biblical texts were held as individual, rather small books stored together in a wooden chest or cupboard. Under such conditions, precisely which works did or did not constitute the Scriptures, or the exact order in which the constituent works should occur, was an irrelevant question. With the invention of the large bound volume, however, which had the immediate practical advantages of compactness and ease of handling and storage, that flexibility of sequence was lost. From then on the books had to come in a specific order – and it is significant that the process of fixing the contents of the Hebrew Bible and of the New Testament coincides historically with the widespread introduction of the codex form. What began as 'the books' had, literally and physically, become 'the book'.

Although the Bible provided Christianity with the medium for both the unity of faith and the unity of culture in late antiquity, the first notable threat to Christian uniformity sprang from the variety of languages in which the Scriptures had been transmitted. Aramaic was the original spoken tongue of Jesus, and its predecessor, Hebrew, was the language of what Christians call the Old Testament. The Old Testament was translated into Greek, probably in the third century BC, for Greek-speaking Jews in Alexandria. Legend has it that 70 (or 72) scholars independently came up with identical translations, hence the name 'Septuagint', or 'Seventy'. The separate books of the New Testament were written in Greek. The complete Bible, both the familiar Old Testament, which had been adopted by the Christians, and the New Testament, were translated from Greek into Latin in an uncontrolled way from the first century onwards. As Greek continued to be used for the Christian liturgy in Rome until the early third century, other centres in Italy or North Africa may have been responsible for these Old Latin versions of the New Testament. At the request of Pope Damasus, St Jerome revised the many versions in use and retranslated the Old Testament from Hebrew. The complete Latin Bible, as revised by St Jerome, is known as the Vulgate. But in the East, Syriac (a type of Aramaic) was the main literary and liturgical language other than Greek, and through Syriac, Christianity was spread to the Far East. The authoritative form of the Bible in the Syriac translation is known as the Peshitta (literally 'simple' or 'widely diffused'). The Peshitta Old Testament was translated from the original Hebrew text, and the Peshitta New Testament from the original Greek. The date of the Peshitta Old Testament is uncertain. It seems likely that most books of the Peshitta Old Testament were translated during the period from the late first century AD to the early third century AD. The Peshitta New Testament is in fact a revision of an earlier translation, known as the Old Syriac. The revision may have been made over a period of time, but was completed sometime in the early fifth century, when the Peshitta eventually replaced the Old Syriac as the authoritative Syriac text.

The Bible in Translations

Armenian is the seventh in the list of languages into which the Bible was translated. But first we must ask why it was translated at all. The answer is that at the heart of the Christian religion is a story which, to the believer, records the most momentous event in history and which he believes it is incumbent on him to make known to the world. That event has to do with the birth, death and resurrection of Jesus the Saviour, with the interpretation of that event and with its consequences in the early decades of what came to be known as the Christian era. The prelude to that event can only be understood by a study of the extraordinary mixture of books which we call the Old Testament – historical literature, prophecy and proverbs, poetry and prose, love lyrics and biography, apocalypse and myth. The central figure who emerges in the four Gospels is given no biography in the sense that we use that word today. Rather, those books present us with glimpses, snapshots as it were, of a figure at once dynamic and gentle, sharp-spoken and tender, wounding and wounded, healing and wooing. The Acts of the Apostles gives a vivid account of the spread of the Christian Church, despite the persecution. The Letters look back on the earthly life and teaching of Jesus of Nazareth, relate that event to life here and hereafter, and meditate on the significance of what happened in that brief period when he walked, worked and suffered among us. The story of the coming together of the twenty-seven books that constitute the New Testament cannot be told here. But it was not very long before the Church went to the world with a book in its hand called the Bible. Indeed, it could not do its missionary work without that book, nor could it offer its worship Sunday by Sunday without readings from it. It was an essential part of its worship and of its outreach to the world.

Hence the need for translations. Where translations were not available or the people were illiterate, pictures on church walls and in church windows – 'the Bible of the poor' – supplemented by miracle plays, proved to be one of the best ways of conveying the message of the faith. Poetry and music contributed to the task. Caedmon, a seventh-century labourer at the monastery of Whitby, discovered that he had the gift of composing verses and, as Bede tells us, 'sang the creation of the world, the origin of men, and all the history of Genesis...the incarnation, passion, resurrection of Our Lord, and his ascension into heaven... He endeavoured to turn away all men from the love of vice, and to excite them in the love of, and application to, good actions.'

2 LEFT The six days of creation and the expulsion of Adam and Eve from Eden, from the Bible of Malnazar and Aghap'ir, Isfahan, 1637–8. *J. Paul Getty Museum, ms. Ludwig I 14, f.2v.*

3 OPPOSITE God the Creator, Adam and Eve in the Garden, and their expulsion from Eden from the Bible by Ghazar, Constantinople, 1646. The two figures fully clothed in red speaking to God represent the patrons of the manuscript. *The British Library, ms. Or.8833, f.2v.*

Who Translated the Bible into Armenian and When?

Armenians call the sacred writings of the Judaeo-Christian tradition that together comprise the Bible 'Astuadsashuntch', which means, 'breath of God'. They have taken St Paul's description of it in 2 Timothy III: 16: 'All Scripture is inspired by God and profitable for teaching, for reproof, for correction, and for training in righteousness, that the man of God may be complete, equipped for every good work.'

That is why they call it the 'breath of God'. If a people has the immortal desire for abundant life, it must go on breathing God's breath, with which it was quickened at the very moment of its creation. This breath can be received through the Word.

At the beginning of the fifth century Armenians felt themselves short of this breath. It is true that Christianity had slowly and quietly spread into Armenia, and, from the times of apostolic evangelization, the seeds of the Gospel took root there and in the course of time spread to adjoining territories. When Gregory the Illuminator started his vigorous campaign to evangelize the whole Armenian people in the late third and fourth centuries, Christianity was not looked upon as an entirely new religion with no known adherents. And the proclamation of Christianity as a state religion around the first quarter of the fourth century was not a shocking surprise. The eminent leaders of the young Church, with the help of Greek and Syrian missionaries, had achieved great success in establishing the new religion. Through the medium of the spoken language, the Gospel was communicated from the earliest period of evangelization to the very beginning of the fifth century.

But hearing the Gospel was not enough to make the impression desired upon the soul. It also had to be read. The need of the written word was felt more and more keenly as time progressed. Nearly a whole century had elapsed since the evangelization of Armenians and still the old pattern of pagan life persisted. The continued presence of pagan beliefs and customs is bewailed by contemporary historians. The historian P'awstos Buzand (425–86) speaks of the presence of idol worship in the south-western district of Taron, the secret devotion to pagan gods, the casting of lots for the purpose of divination and, most of all, the continuation among the upper classes and even at court of pagan funeral practices unbefitting the Christian.

4 The title page of the Armenian Astuadsashuntch (Breath of God) of the Old and New Testaments printed by Mkhit'ar Sebastatsi (1677–1749) on the printing press of Anton Bortoli in Venice, 1733. *The British Library, 17021.d.3.*

In contrast, the Christian is recommended 'not to believe that human death is irreversible and without return once again to life, not to weep and lament excessively in unbridled and hopeless mourning over the departed but rather to look forward with hope toward the coming of the Lord in the hope that each one would receive the eternal reward of his deeds'. In short, as P'awstos Buzand concludes, 'For from antiquity when they had taken on the name of Christians, it was merely as though it were some human religion and they did not receive it with ardent faith, but as some human folly and under duress. They did not receive it with understanding as is fitting, with hope and faith, but only those who were to some degree acquainted with Greek or Syriac learning were able to achieve some partial inkling of it'.

So two saintly and scholarly minds – St Sahak, the Patriarch-Catholicos (*c.* 350–439) and his friend and helper Mesrop Mashtots (*c.* 361–439), who had changed a military career for the life of a monk, missionary, and teacher – undertook the task of carrying out a revolution in the life of the Armenian people. They had a band of zealous men as their collaborators. These men became the pioneers and the leaders of a new awakening. They were called *t'argmanitch*, a Syriac loan word in Armenian, which has a wider connotation than mere 'translator'. They were teachers trained in Edessa, Antioch, Athens and Alexandria, whose principal function had been to render into Armenian orally and *ad hoc* the passages of the scriptures read in church in the Greek or Syriac languages during the services. A 'translator' came to mean a scholar whose calling was to transmit to the people the divine truth through the Bible as well as other religious writings.

In 387, when Armenia came under the control of Zoroastrian Persia, the future course of Armenian Christianity was threatened. If Christianity was to be maintained, it was imperative for the *t'argmanitch* to meet the liturgical and spiritual needs of the Armenian people through the written word. We are fortunate that the story of the invention of the Armenian alphabet and the subsequent translation of the Bible into Armenian is told by three contemporary historians:

(1) Koriwn *vardapet* (*c.* 390–447), whose *Life of Mashtots* – the earliest original writing in Armenian – is the biography of the man who invented the Armenian alphabet in 406.

(2) Ghazar P'arpetsi (*c.* 437–500), whose history covers the period from 387 to 485. In section one he gives his own individual account of the work of Mesrop Mashtots and Sahak in the actual invention of the alphabet and translation of the Bible.

(3) Movses Khorenatsi (*c.* 390–450), who traces Armenian history from its origins to shortly after the death of Mesrop Mashtots. Book III: 52–4 is devoted to the activities of Mesrop.

There is little doubt that the Bible was being used in written form in Armenia prior to the invention of the Armenian alphabet. The question not clearly answered is what language was it written in? According to Ghazar P'arpetsi, 'the worship of the church and the readings of scripture were conducted in Syriac in the monasteries and churches of Armenia'. It appears that Movses Khorenatsi's assertion that 'Armenians did not yet have a script and the church services were conducted in Greek' contradicts the above assertion. However, this detail from Movses refers to the situation in Armenia before its partition in 387. In another context he asserts that after the division 'Persian governors did not allow anyone to learn Greek in their region but only Syriac', while in the Byzantine sector 'where they were subject to the See of Caesarea by virtue of its right of ordination [they] used the Greek script and not Syriac'. The opposition to the use of Greek, according to Movses, had started back in the seventh decade of the fourth century during the rule of Meruzhan Ardsruni, who 'burned whatever books he found', ordered that Persian not Greek letters should be studied, and that no one should speak or translate Greek. Thus, according to Movses, up to the time of the partition the language of the Armenian service was Greek, and after that Syriac. But there is sufficient evidence to suggest that even before that, Syriac was employed alongside Greek, since the southern regions of Armenia had been a zone of Syrian influence for a long time. According to Ghazar, 'the royal scribes at that time conducted the business of the Armenian king's decrees and edicts in Syriac and Greek', while Movses states that 'in the royal court he could find no skilled scribe there, since they used the Persian script'.

It is also relevant to ask in what form the Bible readings were being presented to the masses, for whom both Greek and Syriac were incomprehensible. This is borne out by Ghazar P'arpetsi, who complains, 'the congregations of such a large country were quite unable to comprehend or profit from it because they did not understand the Syrian tongue'. Movses Khorenatsi states that: 'In his teachings the blessed Mesrop endured no little hardship, for he was both reader and translator. And if someone else read when he was not present, it was unintelligible to the people since there was no translator. Therefore, he decided to try to invent letters for the Armenian language'. The historical facts indicate that the books of the Bible, and in particular the Gospels and Psalms on which the entire Christian worship depended, were transmitted by oral translation. The lack of expert translators, the *ad hoc* nature of the translations, and the division of the country into two political zones motivated Sahak and Mesrop to counterbalance political losses with spiritual gains. Soon after the invention of the Armenian alphabet, they set themselves the task of translating the Bible into Armenian. Thus, Armenian literature began with the translation of the Bible.

According to the evidence of the primary sources, the translation of the Bible into classical Armenian was accomplished in two stages. The first translation was done soon after the invention of the Armenian alphabet, between 407 and 412, and the second after the Ecumenical Council of Ephesus in 431, between 433 and 436. According to Koriwn, after Mesrop had invented the Armenian alphabet in the city of Samosata and had it designed by the Hellenic scribe Hrop'anos, Mesrop, together with his pupils Hovhan of Ekegheats and Hovsep' Paghnatsi, 'began the translation of the Bible, first the Proverbs of Solomon, which begins with the exhortation: "To know wisdom and instruction, to perceive the words of understanding".' He completed the translation after his return to Armenia with the help of Sahak. Koriwn testifies 'at that time our blessed and desirable land of Armenia became truly worthy of admiration, where, by the hands of two colleagues, suddenly, in an instant, Moses, the law-giver, along with the order of the prophets, energetic Paul, with the entire phalanx of the apostles, along with Christ's world-sustaining gospel, became Armenian-speaking'.

Movses Khorenatsi, combining these two specific facts from Koriwn's account, seems to suggest that Mesrop began and completed the translation of the Bible: 'Then at once he set to translating into Armenian, wisely beginning with Proverbs, comprising the twenty-two famous books [i.e. the Old Testament] and the New Testament with his collaborators Hovhan of Ekegheats and Hovsep' Paghnatsi'.

After this initial attempt, the early translators – Eznik Koghbatsi, Hovsep' Paghnatsi, Koriwn and Ghewond – were sent to Edessa and Constantinople to learn the art of translation. After the Council of Ephesus, the pupils returned to Armenia in 432 and began the second phase of revising the translation in accordance with the Greek manuscripts they had brought back from Constantinople. Koriwn says 'Sahak, who had translated from the Greek language into Armenian all the liturgical books and the writings of the church fathers, once more undertook, with Eznik, the retranslation of the once hastly done translation on the bases of the authentic (*hastatun*) copies'. The same assertion is also made by Movses Khorenatsi: 'Receiving these [accurate copies of the Scriptures] Sahak and Mesrop zealously translated again what had already been translated and made with them a new version'.

Ghazar P'arpetsi presents the facts in a different manner. He attributes the whole translation of the Bible to Catholicos Sahak Part'ev alone. According to P'arpetsi, after the invention of the Armenian alphabet, Mesrop and his pupils, aware of their lack of expertise and knowledge, approached Sahak with a request to translate the Bible: 'the blessed Mashtots and the honourable priests with him were unable to undertake such a difficult and important task – the translation of the Bible from Greek into Armenian – because they were not sufficiently skilled in the study of Greek', so they 'began to beg the holy Catholicos Sahak to set himself to the spiritual labour of translating the divinely inspired testaments from Greek into Armenian...and when Sahak heard all this...with willing enthusiasm he gave himself to the task, glorying in sharing in the work of God who had given him such grace of knowledge in abundance. Working intrepidly day and night, he translated all the testaments, the utterances of the true prophets, inspired by the holy spirit.'

5 The title page of the Book of Proverbs from an Armenian Bible of the Ghazar Baberdtsi recension, New Julfa, Isfahan, 1661–2. 'To know wisdom and instruction, to perceive the words of understanding' were the first words written in Armenian. They came from the Book of Proverbs, the first part of a translation of the scriptures undertaken between 396 and 430.

This suggests that the translators used a Greek manuscript in two volumes, of which the second began with Proverbs.
The British Library, ms. Or 14101, f.322r.

What was the Armenian Bible Translated From?

The three primary sources on the history of the Armenian Bible (Koriwn, Ghazar P'arpetsi, and Movses Khorenatsi) provide information from three different perspectives, and it is not surprising that diverse opinions have been held concerning the primary base of the Armenian version. Let us look at the evidence of the three authors in the light of the texts.

Soon after the invention of the alphabet 'the blessed ones [Sahak and Mesrop] turned their attention to the improvement and refinement of the literature of their people. Sahak the Great, as before, began to write and to translate'. This statement of Koriwn's is vague and unclear as to what was being translated. Koriwn also records that they sent 'from among their pupils two brothers to the city of Edessa in the region of the Syrians, the first one Hovsep...and the second Eznik...for the purpose of translating and writing down the holy books from Syriac to Armenian'. From this reference to holy books we assume that Koriwn has in mind the books of the Old and New Testaments, which, according to this evidence, were first translated into Armenian from Syriac. In addition, Koriwn says that the seminarians moved 'to the region of the Greeks [i.e. Constantinople], where they joined Eznik and, as most intimate companions, together they performed their spiritual tasks [the work of translating]'. When they had completed their work 'they came to the land of Armenia, having brought authentic copies of the God-given book and many subsequent traditions of the worthy church fathers, along with the canons of Nicaea and Ephesus, and placed before the fathers the testaments of the Holy Church which they had brought with them'.

The 'authentic copies of the God-given book' is a reference to the Septuagint version of the Bible – the Armenian sources never employ the term *Eot'anasnits* (seventy) – which the 'blessed Sahak, who had rendered previously from the Greek language into Armenian all the ecclesiastical books and the wisdom of the Church fathers, once more undertook, with Eznik, the comparison of the former hasty translations with the authentic copies. From this it is clear that up to the Council of Ephesus, held in 431, there was a translation of the Bible done in *p'ut'anaki* ('hasty') fashion, which was improved and perfected after the Council on the basis of 'the authentic copies'.

The evidence about the translation of the Bible provided by Movses Khorenatsi in his *History of the Armenians* is more precise. He records that after the death of the Armenian King Arshak, the Persian King Shapuh dispatched Meruzhan to Armenia to 'convert the land to the Mazdaean religion'. On the road to achieving this he 'attempted to abolish all the institutions of Christianity. The bishops and priests he cast into bonds on the pretext of tribute and had them sent to Persia. Whatever books he found he burned, and he ordered that Greek letters should not be studied, only Persian, and that no one should speak or translate from Greek'. Under such circumstances it was natural for the Armenians to strengthen their ties with Syrian Christian centres, and it is not accidental that Mesrop and his pupils went to Edessa and Amid in search of an Armenian alphabet.

The historian Ghazar P'arpetsi also provides information on the Armenian translation of the Bible, but he wilfully suppresses all knowledge of the existence of a first translation made from Syriac. This is understandable as his writings clearly show that he disliked the Syriac language and culture. He presents the translation accomplished after the Council of Ephesus as being the first. He explains that Mesrop, during his missionary work, had been disadvantaged by the fact that he 'had struggled vainly at the laborious and futile study of Syriac' and 'in his anxiety wept continuously on seeing the great effort and the even greater expense of the young men of Armenia, who at great cost and through long journeys and with continual distractions were spending their days in the schools of Syrian learning. For the worship of the Church and the readings of scripture were conducted in Syriac in the monasteries and churches of the Armenian people. But the congregations of such a large country were quite unable to comprehend or profit from it, and the incomprehension of the Syriac tongue caused labour to the ministers and was unprofitable to the congregations'. This was the reason why soon after the invention of the Armenian alphabet, says Ghazar, 'every soul was ardent for instruction in [written] Armenian, glad that they had been released from the darkness – as it were – of the disability of the Syriac into the light. But they were thrown into uncertainty and were hindered by the lack of Bibles; for the holy testaments of the church did not yet exist in Armenian'. Ghazar concludes that the blessed Mesrop and all the princes of Armenia in concert with the Armenian King Vrampshapuh asked 'the holy Catholicos Sahak to set himself to the spiritual labour of translating the divinely inspired testaments fom Greek into Armenian'.

Evaluating the Most Ancient Authorities

Scores of scholars, both Armenian and foreign, have occupied themselves with the question of which version of the Bible the first and second translations were made from. The principal sources confirm that the post-Ephesus translation, or, more accurately, revision, was done on the basis of authoritative Greek texts brought from Constantinople. Modern scholarship has proved the view first expressed by the nineteenth-century biblical scholar F.C. Conybeare that the Armenian was a version of the Greek Septuagint, 'the text of which everywhere fits closely as a glove the hand that wears it'. The more complex problem, however, seems to be the origin of the first, so-called 'hasty' translation (Armenian 1). While one group of scholars holds the view that it was based on the Greek, another group suggests Syriac, while a third view holds that some books were translated from Greek and others from Syriac. Those who expound the first view rely primarily on the evidence of Koriwn, while those who favour the Syriac origin base their view on the evidence of Movses Khorenatsi who records that after the invention of the Armenian alphabet and missions to Georgia, when Mesrop returned to Armenia he found 'Sahak the Great engaged in translating from Syriac, there being no Greek books available.' The third view, that some books were translated from Greek and others from Syriac is more probable. This is proven not only through manuscript evidence but also textual analysis. It has been shown that some books of the Bible such as Ecclesiasticus, the Song of Songs, I–II Chronicles, and Sirach, have survived in alternative ancient translations in which critics have found traces of the 'hasty' versions. Modern biblical scholars such as Norayr Byuzandatsi, Nerses Akinian and Norayr Pogharian have proved that the book of Ecclesiasticus has survived in two ancient and independent translations as shown in the published texts of Oskan Erevantsi (Amsterdam, 1666) and Hovhannes Zohrapian (Venice, 1805). Equally convincing have been the findings of Hamazasp Oskian regarding the Song of Songs, Grigor Khalateants on I–II Chronicles, and Levon Ter Petrosyan on the Psalms.

When they are dealing with an ancient work in the language in which it was written, scholars endeavour by means of textual criticism to discover the text on which it was based. But in dealing with translations they may have to adopt a quite different procedure. If the translation was an official one from the start, then the task is to determine the original text of the official translation. But the fact is that the official translation very often lies at the end and not at the beginning of the history of the translation of a document from another language.

The term Septuagint, frequently indicated by the Roman numeral sign LXX, is the name not of a version 'but the stamp of authority upon a translation'. St Jerome's Latin version of the Bible, which became the Authorised Version of Western Christendom, was preceded by a large number of individual and unofficial attempts at translation. Because the Christians adopted the Septuagint, the Jews began to avoid it, and about 100 AD they established a standard text, which, after several centuries' revision and editing, became what we now know as the Masoretic text. Following this, a new translation of the Bible into Greek was required for Greek-speaking Jews. The first of these was provided by a man named Aquila in the first half of the second century. His translation not only followed the newly established Hebrew text, but did so with slavish literalness. Towards the end of the second century AD another Jewish proselyte, Theodotion, a native of Ephesus, produced another Greek version of the Old Testament, which was not an original work but a revision of an older Greek translation belonging to the pre-Christian era. It is interesting to note that it was Theodotion's version of Daniel that the Church adopted for its standard version of the Greek Bible in place of the Septuagint version. Some time after Theodotion, another Greek version of the Old Testament was made by Symmachus, who belonged to the Jewish-Christian sect of the Ebionites. His aim seems to have been to provide an idiomatic Greek version, and his method of translation was therefore as far removed as possible from Aquila's. Soon, Greek-speaking Christians also came to feel the need for a standard text of the whole Greek Old Testament. The most important name in the history of the Christian text of the Septuagint is that of the great Alexandrian scholar, Origen (185– 254). In late life, when he had taken up residence at Caesarea in Palestine, Origen produced a masterpiece of biblical learning, which he called the Hexapla (Greek for 'sixfold') because it was an edition of the Old Testament in six parallel columns. The first column contained the Hebrew text in Hebrew script, the second contained the same text transliterated into Greek script, the third and fourth contained the Greek versions of Aquila and Symmachus respectively, the fifth contained Origen's own edition of the Septuagint text, and the sixth contained Theodotion's version.

The manuscript evidence suggests that the Armenian text tradition too is not monolithic but shows textual affinities with the recensions associated with Origen, Lucian of Antioch, Caesarea and Alexandria. Bo Johnson has shown that the Armenian translation of The First Book of Kings is from the recension of Origen. The Göttingen editors of the Septuagint also found the basis of the books of Genesis, Deuteronomy and Jeremiah to belong to the same group as Origen's, while the translations of The Twelve Prophets and the Psalms are traced to the Lucianic text-type. In some individual books scholars have found influences of different recensions. Sahak Kogian, in his textual research into the Books of the Maccabees, came to the conclusion that 'the Armenians had employed the Alexandrian, the Hexapla and Lucianic versions'. Jacques Ziegler found citations of readings in the Armenian text of Ezekiel from 'the Three' (Aquila, Symmachus and Theodotion). These findings of Kogian and Ziegler are confirmed by a colophon in Matenadaran's manuscript No. 193 (dated 1299) to which attention was first drawn by Nerses Akinian: 'This copy is corrected on the basis of the Alexandrian and Jerusalem copies and Origen. The Twelve Prophets were written according to the Septuagint and two translators.'

The presence of Hexaplaric signs in Armenian manuscripts is evidence that the Armenian Old Testament is in many places a witness to the work of Origen. The Armenian version is one of our best sources, alongside certain Greek manuscripts and the Syro-Hexapla: it preserves Origen's signs for some 1462 passages and in slightly more than ten per cent of these cases its witness is unique. The signs are particularly important in establishing what was the original text of the Septuagint. That is, if a certain word or words is 'under the obelus' that is between an obelus (÷) and metabelus (Υ), we know that it is in all likelihood original and not due to some scribal error. On the other hand, if a certain word or words is marked by an asterisk (∗) then we know that Origen added it to the text and that it was therefore not part of the original text.

Similarly, Armenian scribes preserved the work of Aquila, Symmachus and Theodotion in the margins of manuscripts in much the same way as modern translators of the Bible often offer the reader textual notes in the margin. The works of these three ancient translators exist only in fragments, so all evidence of their work is much valued. Armenian manuscripts preserve some 181 readings belonging to Aquila, Symmachus and Theodotion; in two-thirds of the cases, marginal readings are attributed by the abbreviations *ak* (Aquila), *sim* (Symmachus) and *T'* (Theodotion). The majority of the marginal readings (159) are to be found in the books of Samuel and Kings (of which 109 are in 2 Kings); others accompany the text of Joshua, Judges, Job, Isaiah and Ezekiel. It is of particular interest that in some 69 instances the Armenian witness is unique: the evidence is found nowhere else. Armenian manuscripts thus preserve sources that are of crucial interest for textual critics of the Bible. But Origen is not the only source of influence. Lucian (d. 312), contemporary with Origen, also produced a revision of the Septuagint: his version, dominant from the fourth century onwards, lies behind the Armenian translation of Ruth, I–II Samuel (in the Septuagint and Armenian Bible I–II Kingdoms), Chronicles and Daniel.

The status of the New Testament in the Armenian Bible is as complicated as that of the Old. The principal Armenian sources give us no special information in regard to the date and circumstances of an Armenian version of the New Testament. Whatever statements they make apply to it as to Old Testament. It is related by Movses Khorenatsi that the Armenian translators revised the Armenian Bible early in the fifth century on the basis of Greek manuscripts brought from Constantinople. The question remains: what was the date of this earlier version? If we are to believe Movses, who claims that Sahak made it, it will fall as late as about 400. But Movses is not so good a witness as Koriwn or Ghazar, who declare that Sahak translated from Greek. In the face of their evidence we must reject the account of Movses, except where he claims that the earliest Armenian version was made from the Syriac. This could well be the first translation of the Gospels to which the Armenian writer T'eodoros K'rt'enawor (*c.* 600–675) refers in his 'Apology against Mayragometsi' written in 635. In this apology, directed at the Armenian Docetics he declared that 'they [the Docetics] say it was not by weakness but by strength that He [Christ] overcame the enemy. So do His own words testify, the house of the giant is not plundered, unless first the strong man is bound. And if this is true, it is plain, they say, that the first translation is not to be accepted, which in the episode of His praying relates the "Bloody sweat" of the Almighty word of God, and that he was encouraged by the angel.' He continues, 'the letter of the Gospel spoke of the sweat allegorically, as it were of blood; but not as a welling out of blood from a wound made with a weapon.' In the same context we read that the heretics in question contended that the 'old edition of the Gospel is not to be accepted' because it contained verses 43 and

6 The Four Gospels in uncial script of the early tenth century. Folio 118v shows the end of St Mark's Gospel in which the last twelve verses are omitted. The text of verses 7 and 8 is spread out over an entire column on folio 118v, indicating that the scribe was aware of the existence of twelve more verses, and resolved to omit them.
The British Library, ms. Add.21,932. ff.118v-119r.

44 of Luke, Chapter XXII, in which it is related that Jesus was confronted by an angel and sweated drops of blood (some Greek manuscripts omit these verses). They also held that St Gregory the Illuminator, in his homilies on the Gospel oracles which accepts the Divine Word's real suffering, according to God's will, had made no special mention of the 'bloody sweat' passage. The reply of T'eodoros to this argument is that neither did the Nicene Fathers nor the new recensions of the Scriptures recognise more than fourteen Epistles of Paul; yet Gregory the Illuminator had cited and so testified to the III Epistle of the Corinthians to Paul, which the above-mentioned authorities had passed over in silence, and which had not been included in the 'new translation'. The verse cited by Gregory is III Corinthians 11: 'the lawless prince when he desired to be God bound all men under sin'. 'If it be rejected,' says T'eodoros, 'and excluded from the Church because it is not reproduced in the newly circulated translations of the older Gospels, you, in so rejecting it, censure St Gregory.' The drift of the argument is that, just as the Nicene Council ignored an Epistle of Paul, which was yet to be received on the authority of St Gregory, so St Gregory might ignore Luke XXII:43, 44, without prejudicing the authenticity of these verses. The implication of the second argument is much clearer. It is that Gregory had the verses in his translation of the Gospels, but did not quote them because it did not suit his methods of exposition to do so. The implications of these arguments of T'eodoros are very important. It implies that there was an Armenian version, at least of the New Testament, translated from Syriac, for it contained III Corinthians, which stood in the Syriac canon and in no other.

Parts of the New Testament were translated in the fifth century but were omitted from the later Armenian canon. The Revelation of St John, for example, was not read in church before the twelfth century, when Nerses Lambronatsi (1153–98) produced a much-improved recension of the Greek. Similarly, the last twelve verses of Mark were rendered in the fifth century, for Eznik cites them in around 435 but they hardly appear in manuscripts before the thirteenth century, and then not as an integral part of the Gospel of Mark. In 1891 the Armenian scholar F.C. Conybeare (1856–1924) found in the famous Ējmiadsin Gospels written in 989 that the last twelve verses were attributed to 'the Presbyter Ariston', written in small red uncials. Ariston has been identified as Aristion, the teacher of Papias (*c.* 60–130). And the belief that the verses were his and not Mark's explains the hostile attitude towards them in the Armenian Church. The episode of the adulterous woman is likewise absent from the oldest manuscripts, though it is cited by Grigor Narekatsi in 950. The Ējmiadsin manuscript that contains it, though not in the form that Grigor and the later codices have it, gives it as follows: 'A certain woman was taken in sins, against whom all bore witness that she was deserving of death. They brought her to Jesus [to see] what he would command, in order that they might malign him. Jesus made answer, and said, "Come you, who are without sin, cast stones, and stone her to death." But he himself, bowing his head, was writing with his finger on the earth to declare their sins; and they were seeing their several sins on the stones. And, filled with shame, they departed, and no one remained, but only the woman. Said Jesus, "Go in peace, and present the offering for sins, as in their law is written."'

August Merk has compiled a table of about 200 readings from the Gospels alone, where the Armenian version agrees with the Syriac against the Greek. Here are a few instances:

(1) Matthew IV: 18. Greek version: 'While Jesus walked by the sea of Galilee.' Armenian version: 'While Jesus walked by the shore of the sea of Galilee.' The word *ezr*, meaning 'shore' (Syriac *yad*) occurs only in the Armenian.
(2) Matthew V:23. Armenian version: 'Remember if your brother has *khet*' against you.' The Armenian *khet* (Syriac *akta*) does not feature in the Greek (it has 'something').
(3) Mark I:44. Armenian version: 'Go and offer *patarag* (sacrifice) for your cleansing.' The Armenian *patarag* (Syriac *qurbana*) does not appear in the Greek.
(4) Luke II:49. Armenian version: 'Did you not know that I ought to be in my father's house.' Greek version: 'I ought to be in my father's.' The Armenian and Syriac versions include the word for 'house', but it does not appear in Greek – it is simply understood. Levon Ter Petrosyan lists around 100 instances of Syriacisms in the Psalms.

It remains to point out that the Armenian is not the only version to show traces of the older Syriac text. F.C. Conybeare was of the view that the Georgian version also shows a considerable number of Syriacisms, which, like the Armenian, seems to have been originally based on an old Syriac text and afterwards remodelled according to Greek manuscripts. But whereas the remodelling of the Armenian was done by Sahak and Mesrop early in the fifth century, the Georgian version was not made until the 11th century by St Euthymius (d. 1026) on Mount Athos. Modern scholars, such as Robert Blake, Stanislaus Lyonnet, Gérard Garitte and Akaki Shanidze, have concluded that the earliest Georgian translation was done from the Armenian and regard the relationship between the Armenian and the Georgian as that of 'parent and daughter'. This affinity is particularly noticeable in the case of the Gospels, the Acts of the Apostles and the Psalms in which they have found not inconsiderable agreement with the Armenian. Among these affinities, the most striking are the mistranslations found in the Georgian, which can only be explained by the Armenian text. For example, in St Matthew's Gospel XXI: 12 and John II: 15 the Greek word for 'money changers' has been rendered into the Armenian word *hatavachar*, then translated into Georgian as *t'eslis mop'ardult'ay* (seed-seller). Here the Georgian translator has misunderstood the Armenian word *hat*, which has the double meaning of 'seed' and 'part.' In Matthew XIV: 1 the Georgian translates the words for 'Herod the tetrarch' as *Herodes tchorordi*, which is a transliteration of the Armenian term *tchorordapet*. Modern scholars are more inclined to explain the Syriac influences as a result of the acquaintance of the Armenian translators with the pre-Peshitta version, the Diatessaron of Tatian: a Harmony of the Gospels, in which a single narrative was constructed from the four separate Gospels, and Ephrem's Commentaries. The discovery of both Diatessaronic sequences of harmonization and Diatessaronic variants the oldest strata of Armenian Gospel text is attributable to the Armenian translation of St Ephrem the Syrian's *Commentary on the Diatessaron* in the fifth century. In 1954 Louis Leloir published the Armenian text of Ephrem's *Commentary on the Diatessaron* with a parallel Latin translation.

The Influence of the Vulgate

In 1818 William G. Goodell of the American Missionary Society popularized the view that beginning in the thirteenth century, during the reign of King Hetum II, the 'unadulterated' text of the Armenian Bible was corrupted by 'Jerome's prefaces and many alterations and corruptions from the Vulgate'. But modern research has proved conclusively that such a view is based on a misinterpretation. If we go behind the 1666 edition of Oskan Erevantsi's Bible, which was the source of William Goodell's opinion, we will see that the impact of the Latin Vulgate is considerably limited and it all originated from Oskan's edition, revision and alteration of the text on the basis of the Vulgate. But because Oskan used King Hetum's famous Bible manuscript dating from 1295, now in the Institute of Ancient Manuscripts in Matenadaran (ms. No. 180) researchers had wrongly assumed that the revisions were attributable to this manuscript text. In fact Hakob Anasyan and Suren K'olandjyan have proved the revisions to be the work of Oskan. Manuscript 180 has preserved all the marginal annotations made by Oskan, which were then incorporated into the printed edition. The text of the manuscript is that of the authentic classical Armenian version. There is, however, one influence from the Vulgate that cannot be denied. It is the division of the text into chapters. This division was introduced by the English Archbishop Stephen Langton, who died in 1228. By the fourteenth century the Latin chapters begin to appear in some

Armenian manuscripts. From the middle of the seventeenth century, this division is made more explicit by the use of the letter 'F' (Frank meaning Latin), especially in the manuscripts of the New Julfa scriptorium, where regular debates on the Scriptures took place between Latin, Jewish, Armenian and Islamic theologians, and the need to quote the Scriptures by chapter and verse was an obligation.

By the third decade of the fifth century, therefore, the text of the Armenian Bible was already fixed and should be named the 'Sahak-Mesropian version', the canonical and authentic text of the Armenian church. Parallel to the written text there also existed the oral tradition,

7 The title-page of the Armenian Bible edited by Oskan Erevantsi (1614–74) printed in 'Holy Ējmiadsin and St Sargis' press in Amsterdam 1666–68. This is the first printed edition of the Bible in classical Armenian. It comprises 1462 double-column pages with 159 illustrations. *The British Library, Or.70.bb.2.*

which persisted for a long period. The historian Ghazar P'arpetsi writes that 'Our blessed teachers taught us the whole of the covenant of the church three and four times from the beginning to the end of the book, demanding the same from us, and forced us to repeat it like the psalms of David.' According to Catholicos Babken Kiwlesērian (1868–1936) the practice of learning the Four Gospels and the Psalms to recite orally 'without stumbling, as if from a book, during worship…had not yet replaced the oral tradition'. Ghazar P'arpetsi refers to a variation of Psalm XVI:14 which reads: 'They were sated with food – which another translator calls pork.' The similarity of the Greek words *huon* (pigs) and *huion* (sons) has given rise to this confusion. The evidence of T'eodoros K'rt'enawor in his 'Apology against the Mayragometsi' that the Armenian Docetics hold that 'the First translation is not to be accepted', is proof that in the early centuries textual purity was a concern of Armenian criticism. The Zohrabian edition (1805), like the Authorized King James Version (1611), has 'whose belly thou fillest with thy hid treasure…and leave the rest to their sons' (Psalm XVI [17]:14).

That the value of the Sahak-Mesropian translation was recognized in the medieval period is supported by Gospel ms. No. 10434 (dated 1069), the colophon of which asserts that it was copied from an exemplar copy written by Mesrop. The receiver of the manuscript, Anania Varagatsi, gives so much importance to this belief that he claims his manuscript is worth the whole world. 'In the Armenian era 518, I, Anania Varagatsi, the unworthy priest and the humblest among the wise…gave this Holy Gospel to be copied by the scribe Yovhannes and acquired it through my own means, which I regard more valuable than the whole world…particularly for its authenticity, since, according to tradition, it was written by St Mesrop, *vardapet* and translator…' From this perspective the following colophon, which describes the efforts of Yovhannes the Philosopher to discover the most authentic text of the Psalter, is also relevant: 'This deacon, a holy man, a visionary, was in great pain for a long period for the corruption of the Psalter and could not find a way of correcting the text. Then, searching the boxes of books in the monastery of Haghbat, among the many manuscripts he found the translator's version of the Psalter.'

8 The title-page of the Book of Genesis from the Bible by Ghazar, Constantinople, 1646. The portraits of the four Evangelists with their symbols adorn the corners of the headpiece, while the Virgin and Child are placed in the centre.
The British Library, ms. Or.8833, f.3r.

The Canon of the Bible

The word 'canon', from the Greek *kanon*, meaning 'norm' or 'standard', is common to all religious traditions and refers to an authoritative corpus of writings considered normative for faith. In this sense, the word appears to have been first used by St Athanasius in his *Decrees of the Synod of Nicaea* (*c.* 350). The traditional view is that the Pentateuch, or Torah, was 'canonized' at an assembly of rabbis meeting towards the end of the first century AD in Jamnia, a town west of Jerusalem. The books included in the whole Bible were divided into three main groups: Law or Torah (the first five books of the Bible, also known as the Pentateuch); Prophets; and Writings (Hagiographa). The Septuagint, although now rejected by the Jews, survived in use as the Old Testament of the Bible used by the Greek Church. The books it contains, in various subsequent translations, were inherited by all Christian churches until the Reformation in the sixteenth century, when the Protestant Reformers, anxious for the verbal accuracy of their translations, went back to the Hebrew text. In the process, books included in the Septuagint (the canon of the Alexandrian Jews), but excluded from the Hebrew canon, came to be relegated to a secondary section, usually referred to as the Apocrypha, and not normally included in Protestant Bibles. Thus, the Old Testament of a Protestant Bible will usually contain fewer books than those of an Orthodox or Catholic Bible. The order of contents common to all will also differ for this reason.

The earliest translations into Latin, made to serve the Christian communities in the western provinces of the Roman empire, never achieved official status or even uniformity. The textual variety that could be found in individual copies of the Bible was already a cause for concern in the fourth century. Pope Damasus I (304–84) commissioned St Jerome (*c.* 340–420) to revise the Latin translation. Jerome's revision of the New Testament was ready in 384. For the Old Testament, however, he was not satisfied simply with revision of a translation made from the Septuagint, but preferred to go back to the original Hebrew, where it existed. In this work he was aided by a number of Jewish rabbis. As Jerome said, 'Let him who would challenge aught in this translation ask the Jews.' Jerome's translation established itself as the standard version in Western Europe by the seventh century. The title Vulgate, from the Latin *vulgatus*, meaning 'common', or 'widespread', was declared authoritative by Pope Clement VIII in 1592 at the Council of Trent.

The Canon of the Armenian Bible

The growth of the Armenian canon is complex because the evidence available is far from complete and there is no clear and consistent conception of canonicity. Movses Khorenatsi, describing the literary activities of Mesrop Mashtots in Samosata, writes, 'completing the twenty-two unhidden books, he also translated the New Testament into Armenian'. The twenty-two unhidden books correspond to the books of the Hebrew canon. The second reference comes in the form of an instruction attached to Canon XXIV of the Council of Partav summoned in 768 by Catholicos Sion I Bawonetsi: 'And to you all, clergy and laymen, the books to be revered from the Old and New Testaments are these:

Moses' Book of Genesis	II Ezra
Exodus	Book of Job
Leviticus	I Book of Psalms
Numbers	III Solomon
Deuteronomy	XII Prophets
Joshua Son of Nun	Isaiah
Judges and Ruth	Jeremiah
I–IV Kingdoms	Ezekiel
II Chronicles	Daniel

And outside these we decree for instruction of your children the study of the Wisdom of Sirach.'

The books categorized by the Council of Partav as 'revered' corresponds to the twenty-two books of the Hebrew canon, except that their enumeration and sequence is different. It is interesting that the instruction draws a distinction between those books that are 'revered' and those that are 'outside'. Those classed as 'revered' are used during liturgy and worship, which is one of the most crucial factors in deciding the limits of the canon. The Book of Sirach is classed as 'outside' these and confined to catechetical instruction. This is the only list we have of the books of the Old Testament canon in Armenian, but it may have Conciliar legitimacy. However, Archbishop Norayr Pogharian (1904–) has published two texts of identical content found in the Epistle of St Clement and in ms. No.1104 of St James's Collection, and suggests that all three may conceivably derive from catechetical teaching. His reasons are: (1) All three mention in their headings the intention to enumerate the canonical books of the Old Testament as well as the New, but all three fail to inform on the books of the New Testament. It is inconceivable that all three have lost this information by accident and independently of each other. (2) All three exclude from the Old Testament the Book of Esther. (3) All three include the Book of Sirach for catechetical teaching. This leads us to draw the conclusion that the Council of Partav did not concern itself with the question of the canon of the Bible and, therefore, did not formulate the limits of the canon. If it had, it would have been a separate clause which

would have dealt with not only the Old Testament but also with the New Testament. The clause in its present form is an unlearned addition to the canons of the Council of Partav made by a copyist who had as his source an older text. Therefore, this text cannot be said to represent the official position of the Armenian church on the status of the canon of the Bible.

The third authentic source of information for the Armenian canon is the Book of Rituals (*Mayr Mashtots*), which contains scriptural readings for the ordination of the Catholicos, the Bishop and blessing of the holy chrism (oil). At the ordination rite of the Bishop, the Catholicos asks the prospective candidate the question: 'The Old and the New Testaments, which were given by the grace of the Holy Spirit through the hands of the prophets and apostles, do you vow to lead your flock by these alone and to instruct them by these alone...?' He then reads the following list:

1.	Genesis	10.	I–II Chronicles
2.	Exodus	11.	Job
3.	Leviticus	12.	Solomon
4.	Numbers	13.	David
5.	Deuteronomy	14.	Isaiah
6.	Joshua	15.	Jeremiah
7.	Judges	16.	Ezekiel
8.	Ruth	17.	Daniel
9.	I–IV Kingdoms	18.	XII Prophets

We understand that the three books attributed to Solomon – Proverbs, Song of Songs and Wisdom – when added to the seventeen will give twenty. The missing books that would make up the twenty-two are Esther and Ezra-Nehemiah. This listing of the books according to the threefold groupings of Law, Prophets and Writings is ancient and has major importance in the delimitation of the Armenian canon.

The Armenian author Anania Shirakatsi (615–690) has a stichometry (word count) of the books of the Old and New Testaments. It includes the books of Nehemiah and Revelation, but does not indicate their counts, which suggests that these books were read for instruction but not revered. Nowadays, although the Book of Revelation is part of the canon, it is never read in church, and not a single reading is included in the

Armenian lectionary (list of scriptures to be read at divine services). Unfortunately, we do not have a manuscript of the Bible from Anania Shirakatsi's period to check whether this was a stage in the progress of the Armenian canon or if Shirakatsi was just translating a work from Greek.

The third listing that has come down to us is preserved in the Bible of Mkhit'ar Ayrevanetsi (1222–1290) copied in 1285 by Yovhannes *Vanakan*. The enumeration and arrangement of the books in that manuscript follows Anania Shirakatsi's listing. Finally, Grigor Tat'evatsi, when asked in his *Book of Questions*, 'How many and which are the books of the Old and New Testaments?' suggests his own listing (see appendix 2).

The Christian Church adopted the twenty-two books of the Jewish canon and added the 'ecclesiastical' books specified by Athanasius. These were the Wisdom of Solomon, Sirach, Judith, Tobit and Esther and the four books of the Maccabees. The early Church Fathers were reluctant to add any books that Origen called Apocrypha, meaning 'hidden' or 'withheld from general circulation', because they contained esoteric lore suitable only for the initiated. Among these were the Prayer of Joseph, the Story of Joseph and Asenath, and the Testaments of the twelve patriarchs, to mention only those that are regularly found in Armenian manuscripts. At a later stage the term 'apocrypha' came to denote un-canonical books, particularly in the Protestant tradition, while in the Catholic Church the Council of Trent (1546) and the Vatican Council (1870) called them 'deutero-canonical'. To present the enumeration and arrangement of the books of the Old Testament in the Armenian Bible we enlist the contents of three of the earliest listings. The first list contains the four books of the Maccabees, while the other two lists have only three. None of the extant manuscripts have all four books of the Maccabees. Two of the lists have the Testaments and the Deaths of the Patriarchs, a characteristic that is unique to all the Armenian manuscripts. One has the Book of Enoch, which is very rare in manuscripts, but the Story of Joseph and Asenath, very common in Armenian manuscripts, is missing from these lists. Two

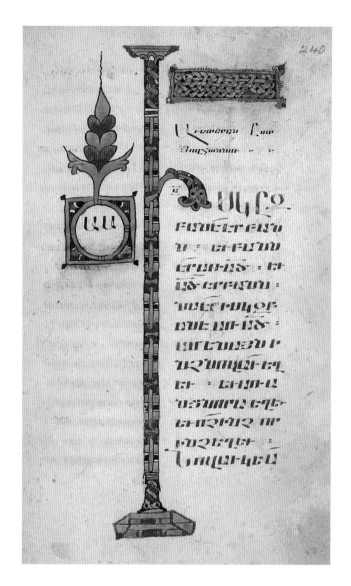

9 The headpiece of St John's Gospel, from the Four Gospels of 1166. The verse numbers of each Gospel appear in the margin surrounded by square ornaments in green ink.
The British Library, ms. Add.19727, f.240r.

of the lists have the Book of Baruch. On the whole the Armenian canon of the Old Testament follows the Greek Septuagint, so it includes Ezra II, Judith, Tobith, Sirach and Maccabees, adding to these the Testaments, the Deaths of the Patriarchs and the Story of Joseph and Asenath.

The New Testament

From the late first century into the early second, Christian writings, along with the Old Testament scriptures, were consulted for handling disputes or matters related to worship and ministry practices of the church in some communities. Even without a special word for it, we can unmistakably see the existence of the authorized collection of holy writings, *graphai*, in the first Christian communities. In his letters, Paul frequently refers to 'the writing' as the source material for illustration and argument, and takes it for granted that his readers will know what he is talking about. In Judaism the notion of sacred literature can be seen in IV Ezra, where he refers to a collection of ninety-four books sacred to the Jews. Twenty-four of these were for everyone, but seventy were reserved for the wise among the people.

From the second century to the middle of the fifth century, rabbis were discussing which documents belonged among the sacred collection of Scriptures and which did not ('defiled the hands'). The rabbinic definition of the canon was done partly in a polemical atmosphere against the Christian community: the books most often appealed to by Christians (II Esdras, Sirach), were specifically omitted as books that did not 'defile the hands'.

What notion of sacred books came to be applied to writings by Christians? How did Christians set about defining their canon as the Jews had defined theirs? II Peter III:16 strongly suggests that Paul's letters, or some of them, were included in a Christian collection of sacred writings by the time the Epistle was written: the author speaks of the problems people have in interpreting Paul's work, and of the way in which the unscrupulous distort Paul's theology, 'just as they do with the rest of the *graphai*'. II Peter is most unlikely to be earlier than AD 100, but it can hardly be much later than 125, so this is probably the earliest evidence we have for a collection of Christian 'scripture'. The anonymous sermon long known as the Second Letter of Clement, written between 130 and 150, refers to Matthew's Gospel as *graphe*, so that it seems as if one or more Gospels and at least some of Paul's letters formed the nucleus of a Christian canon by the middle of the second century. Obviously, this did not happen overnight; and, indeed, if we look through the surviving Christian literature of the early second century, we can see that even before the idea of a new Christian canon appears, there was already a certain degree of consensus about the status of some writings: they were quoted, or at least echoed, in works from all around the Mediterranean. They might not have been regarded as holy or inspired by God in the same way as the Jewish scripture, but they had a 'classical' standing, expressing the fundamental truths of Christian belief in a way recognizable to a wide variety of people. They had begun to shape a common language for Christians.

The pressure to decide on canonical limits to Christian writings was acute by the end of the second century. The Christian Churches had never been monolithic, but the growth of groups within and on the margin of the churches, which took an exceptionally radical line on the Church's relation to Jewish scripture, prompted the question of acceptable limits to diversity. Early in the second century there began to appear an ever-growing stream of pseudepigraphical and apocryphal Christian writings in the form of letters, gospels, apocalypses and acts. Each of these claimed to be the work of one or other of the Apostles. As the second century wore on, this stream became a veritable flood. This practice of pseudepigraphy ran riot in the final quarter of the second century. Before long a whole 'New Testament' of works bearing the name of Paul, Peter or almost any other Apostle could have been collected. The Church at Rome held certain writings to be Apostolic – namely those being read in its services of worship. The creation of the New Testament by that Church was the result of its effort to protect these documents. The limits of the New Testament were meant to serve as dykes to keep out the flood of secondary literature. In its conflict with Gnosticism in the middle of the second century, the Church at Rome had drawn a sharp line between the Apostolic and the post-Apostolic ages. This division was now brought out to measure the literature of the Christian movement. Those writings that met the test were accepted; those that failed were rejected. What the Church at Rome actually did between 170 and 180 was only to ratify the position that the accepted writings had already achieved for themselves. The division excluded the great mass of acts and lives of the martyrs. The inclusion of 'Apostolic' writings and the rejection of all others gave this collection the character of a canon – making these writings the 'books of the new covenant'. The decision of the Roman Church is recorded in the Muratorian canon (Rome, *c.* 200). The formal recognition of New Testament literature as scripture is first attested by Irenaeus of Lyons (*c.* 180–190), who appears to have been the first to use the terms 'Old Testament' and 'New Testament' to distinguish the Hebrew scriptures from the Christian sacred writings. After him, there was widespread acceptance of many New Testament writings as scripture, especially by Christian apologists Justin Martyr (*c.*100–165), Tertullian in North Africa (*c.*160–255), Clement of Alexandria in Egypt (*c.* 150–*c.* 215), Origen (*c.* 185–*c.* 254), Hippolytus (*c.* 170–*c.* 236), Athanasius (*c.* 296–373) and others. Thus the many church fathers had pretty well defined the contents and position of the New Testament canon. Now it was up to the councils to put the final stamp of approval on views about the New Testament that already prevailed.

In 303, the Emperor Diocletian launched the last great persecution against the Christians. In the first of four edicts, he demanded that the churches be destroyed and their sacred scriptures be confiscated and burned. Many Christians were persecuted and put to death because of their refusal to hand over their sacred books, and one can assume that individual Churches had already identified which books were demanded. Those who gave in and handed over these books were called *traditores* or *lapsi* ('the fallen'). Those who refused were called 'confessors'. And those who died for refusing to turn them over were called 'martyrs'. Although the Churches were not in complete agreement on which books were sacred, it is likely that most of them had by then decided the broad parameters of their biblical canon.

The conversion of Emperor Constantine (?285–337) brought many benefits to the Church, not least of which was the cessation of persecution and the opportunity to move towards unity in theology and the biblical canon. Constantine requested Eusebius (*c.* 260–*c.* 340) to produce fifty copies of the scriptures for use in the new capital city of Constantinople. Which books to include in those copies was probably decided by Eusebius, but his choice was accepted by the emperor, a fact that would probably influence other Christians' decisions on the matter.

Around 325, Eusebius established three categories for Christian books: those that were 'accepted' as scripture, those that were 'questionable' or 'disputed', and those that were 'spurious'. He included in the first group twenty of the current New Testament books (the four Gospels, Acts, thirteen epistles of Paul, I John, and I Peter. The 'questionable' group – James, II Peter, Jude, II and III John, and possibly Hebrews and Revelation – was not part of Eusebius's own biblical canon. The spurious group, which included the Gospels of Peter, Thomas and Matthias, the Acts of Andrew, Paul and John, the Didache, and the Apocalypse of Peter, was rejected outright. In time, the 'questionable' books were accepted by most Churches, but the third group failed to find acceptance. The smaller canon closely approximated the canon accepted in the Syriac-speaking Church in the fourth and fifth centuries.

The Council of Laodicea, held in Asia Minor in 363, forbade the reading of books that were not canonical. The last canon (No. 60) contains a list of all the present New Testament books with the exception of the Revelation of John. The Council of Hippo in North Africa in 393 included only the present New Testament writings as scripture. Four years later, in 397, the Council of Carthage registered the sacred writings belonging to the New Testament, an enumeration which is exactly that of our New Testament today – although Hebrews was not at this time included among the letters of Paul. It was not until the next Council of Carthage, in 419, that Hebrews was listed among the Pauline letters and the listings of the earlier council were reaffirmed.

The Armenian Canon of the New Testament

The ancient Armenian writers give us no special specific information on the Armenian canon. Koriwn speaks in general terms of St Paul's 'fourteen epistles' and acknowledges the canon of the Bible in terms of its divisions – the Law, the Prophets, the Epistles and the Gospels. The clause attached to Canon XXIV of the Council of Partav lists the books of the Old Testament but not those of the New Testament. Much recent discussion has revealed that the passage in the canons of the Council of Partav is an incomplete extract taken from Clement of Alexandria's book *The Outlines* [of scripture]. The first complete listings of the New Testament books are found (as detailed on pages 25 and 26) in the stichometry of Anania Shirakatsi, followed by listings attributed to Hovhannes Sarkavag and Grigor Tat'evatsi.

Of these three lists outlining the development of the Armenian canon, the most interesting is that of Grigor Tat'evatsi whose collection of books includes six disputed ones: the Doctrine Addai or the Acts of Thaddaeus, Apocrypha of James, Didache, Acts of Justus, Dionysius Areopagite and the Acts of Peter. We simply do not know what prompted Grigor Tat'evatsi to incorporate these disparate books among the authorized ones, other than to match the number of the books in the New Testament with that of the Old Testament. Or perhaps he was simply attempting to marry the number of books with the thirty-six letters of the Armenian alphabet. Whatever the case, we cannot find any of these books in Armenian biblical manuscripts, even the Acts of Thaddeus (chief apostle of the Armenian Church). A common feature of the two lists attributed to Hovhannes Sarkavag and Tat'evatsi and to the majority of manuscripts is the inclusion of the Epistle of the Corinthians to Paul and a Third Epistle of Paul to the Corinthians. Both were in use in the Armenian Church as late as the thirteenth century. The existence of III Corinthians was first made known to European scholars through an Armenian manuscript from Smyrna to which Archbishop James Ussher called attention in 1644. From this manuscript, which is incomplete, David Wilkins (1685–1745), Librarian at Lambeth Palace, published the Armenian text with a Latin translation (Amsterdam, 1715). William and George Whiston, sons of William Whiston, the translator of Jewish historian Josephus (*c.* 37–*c.* 100), included the Armenian text, with a Latin and Greek translation, in an Appendix to their *History of Moses of Chorene* [Khoren] (London, 1736.) Lord Byron made an English translation of the Epistle and published it with the original texts in his *Armenian Grammar and Chrestomathy* (Venice, 1819). This Epistle was included in the Armenian canon primarily for theological consideration as it contains explicit testimony in support of its doctrine of 'ascended into heaven with the same body' and 'is to come with the same body'. T'eodoros K'rt'enawor in his *Apology against the Mayragometsi* (see page 23) confirms that III Corinthians belonged to the first translation of the New Testament, for it was cited by St Gregory the Illuminator, and also supported by Koriwn, who attributes 'fourteen Epistles' to St Paul.

It is true to say that the Armenian Church fathers were well aware of the existence of the non-canonical books of the Old and New Testaments, which had all been rendered into Armenian, but during the gradual process of establishing the canon, some came to be viewed as unorthodox and non-canonical and were excluded. The fathers were aware of the debates, and to support their selection of books they also translated the available supporting literature. The canonicity of III Corinthians was supported by the translation into Armenian of *St Ephrem's Commentary*, where Paul explicitly favours the doctrine of the Resurrection and Second Coming of Christ as being 'with the same body'. For this same reason the Epistle to the Hebrews is always prefaced with the note: 'The Epistle to the Hebrews had not been attributed to Paul on the basis of its style and because it does not bear his name.'

Recensions of the Armenian Bible

It is important to note that the earliest specimens of the Bible are selections of individual books: the Pentateuch, the Prophets, the four Gospels, the Psalms, and the Epistles of Paul. The large, majestic uncial script was not suitable for the production of the whole Bible in a single volume. The emergence of the more economical *bolorgir* script solved this problem, and by the close of the twelfth century, Nerses Lambronatsi (1153–98) compiled the first complete recension of the Bible books. The colophon of a Bible manuscript (Matenadaran ms. No.177) dated 1289, copied by the scribe Movses Erznkatsi, praises Lambronatsi's literary activity, citing in particular his 'collecting together of the books of the Bible, leaving behind him an accomplishment worthy of benevolent envy, since up to his time such a compilation had not been put together in our nation'. The few complete Bibles that have survived from the thirteenth century bear witness to Erznkatsi's comment.

The second recension is attributed to Gevorg Skevratsi (1246–1301), who also introduced prefaces and chapter contents to the individual books of the Bible. This is affirmed by several colophons found in manuscripts. A relevant passage in his Biography records that he 'introduced into the Bible prefaces and chapter headings which the former fathers had ignored'. During Skevratsi's time, however, the chapter and verse divisions of the Latin Vulgate proved more influential. They were introduced by Stephen Langton, a lecturer at the University of Paris, later Archbishop of Canterbury. A comparison of the two shows significant variations.

The Latin Genesis has fifty chapters, while the Armenian has fifty-eight, and the Latin Exodus has forty chapters, while the Armenian has 169. The Latin concordance numbers introduced to Armenian manuscripts of the fourteenth century simplify the comparative study of the Latin and Armenian texts. This innovation was credited to King Het'um, whose Bible, with his hand-written annotations in the margins, has survived. The colophon which sheds light on this innovation states: 'The Latin numbers, which are called *jabistr* (chapters), cover the whole Bible. I Het'um, who is also called John, after hard labour had it changed in order that it would be easier to find the parallels in both texts.' Thus the Book of Genesis has fifty headings and the letters 'F' and 'R' indicate Frank [i.e. Latin].' This recension of Gevorg Skevratsi acquired wide circulation and influence in Cilician and Armenian monasteries, and the three primary printed editions of Oskan Erevantsi (Amsterdam, 1666), Hovhannes Zohrabian (Venice, 1805) and Arsen Bagratuni (Venice, 1860) were based on this recension.

In the seventeenth century the development of modern chapter and verse divisions filtered into Armenian manuscripts. The verse numberings worked out for the Hebrew concordance of the Masoretic text by Rabbi Isaac Nathan in about 1440 first appear in an Armenian manuscript of the Bible (Mat. No. 351) copied in Lvov in 1619 on the request of Ghazar Baberdtsi. This third recension of the Bible in Armenian was popular and widely copied by the scribes in Isfahan.

Printed Editions of the Armenian Bible

'In the beginning was the Word, and the Word was with God, and the Word was God... In him was life; and the life was the light of men. And the light shineth in darkness.' (John I:1–5)

From the middle of the fifteenth century, the word of God, which had been limited for the most part to monks in abbeys and monasteries and priests in the churches, spread throughout Western Europe with the invention of printing. Johannes Santritter, in his 1483 edition of Eusebius's *Chronicon*, notes in the entry for 1457:

'For a method of printing was devised in 1440 by the clever genius of Johann Gutenberg, a knight of Mainz. In this time, it has been extended to almost all parts of the world. The whole of antiquity, being collected in small pieces of brass [type], is read by posterity in an infinite number of volumes.'

This is thought to be the earliest written acknowledgement of Gutenberg as the inventor of the movable type printing process in the West. His forty-two-line Bible, printed probably in 1454 or 1455, is acknowledged as the first complete book printed by this method. If we are to accept 1440 as the date for the beginning of printing, then Gutenberg laboured fifteen years to perfect the design of his typeface, the process of punching matrices and casting re-usable type, of setting pages and organizing quires, of developing resources, such as his paper supply, and developing a production schedule. It is thanks to Gutenberg's invention that the Bible has been so widely disseminated during the past 500 years.

With a zeal similar to that of the 'holy translators', Armenian church leaders in the sixteenth century, recognizing the utility of the new invention, campaigned hard to introduce printing to Armenia. The Armenian Catholicos Azaria of New Julfa (1584–1601), encouraged by the efforts of the first Armenian printer, Hakob Meghapart, who had set up a press in Venice and published the first six Armenian books between 1509 and 1513, wrote to Pope Gregory XIII in 1585, asking for support to print an Armenian Bible in Venice. That support never materialized, but the project eventually came about thanks to the financial support of wealthy Armenians. The rapid progress of printing in the

10 The title-page of St John's Gospel from the Bible by Malnazar and Aghap'ir, New Julfa, Isfahan, 1637–8. The opening word '*iskzbanē*' is in large, coloured bird capitals, with the evangelist's symbol, the Eagle, forming the letter 'I'. It is followed by three lines of small *erkat'agir* script, and continued in small *bolorgir* script. The Ammonian canons are added in the lower and lateral margins.
J. Paul Getty Museum, ms. Ludwig I 14, f.537v.

diaspora coincided with the appearance of prosperous Armenian communities outside the homeland. It was this factor that assisted Armenian clerics to set up printing houses in Venice (1509), Paris (1537), Constantinople (1567), Rome (1579), New Julfa (1636), Amsterdam (1660), Livorno (1670) and many other capitals. Khatchatur Kesaratsi (1590–1646), the pupil of eminent scholars Grigor Kesaratsi and Movses Tat'evatsi, became prelate of the New Julfa diocese in 1620. Having been denied permission to establish a printing press in Rome to print an Armenian Bible, he set one up in New Julfa in 1636, the first press in Persia and western Asia, where he printed the Psalms, the only known copy of which is now in the Bodleian Library, Oxford. Having printed three more titles between 1639 and 1642, he began printing the Bible in 1650, but, according to the evidence of the traveller Jean Baptiste Tavernier in 1655, this remained incomplete. Prior to the printing of the first Bible, the Psalter had already been printed twelve times:

> Venice, 1512–13, Hakob Meghapart
> Venice, 1566, Abgar T'okhat'etsi
> Venice, 1587, Yovhannes Terzntsi
> Lvov, 1616, Yovhannes K'armatanetsi
> New Julfa, 1636–38, Khatchatur Kesaratsi
> Venice, 1642, Yovhannes Ankiwratsi
> Livorno, 1644, Yovhannes Jughayetsi
> Venice, 1660, Sahak and Step'anos
> Amsterdam, 1662, Mat'eos Dsaretsi
> Amsterdam, 1664, Oskan Erevantsi
> Venice, 1666, Jean.B. Povis
> Amsterdam, 1666, Karapet Andrianatsi

During the catholicate of P'ilippos I Aghbaketsi (1633–55), the Dominican brothers John and Paul Piromalli were in Ējmiadsin between 1642 and 1647. They befriended Oskan Erevantsi (1614–74), who later, with the support of wealthy Armenian patrons, founded a press in Amsterdam and inaugurated a golden age of book production with the printing in 1666 of the first complete Armenian Bible. The text of his Bible was based on a single manuscript copied for King Het'um II in 1295, now preserved in the Institute of Ancient Manuscripts (Matenadaran) as ms. 180. The Oskanian Bible, comprising of 1,462 double pages with 159 illustrations

by the Dutch artist Christoffel van Sichem, was, everyone agrees, an outstanding achievement. Oskan Erevantsi's desire to see the Bible printed led him to make changes and corrections in the classical Armenian text to comply with the demands of Catholic censorship. In his assessment of Oskan's Bible, the Armenian historian Mikael Tchamtchian (1738–1823) says, 'When Paul the cleric [i.e. Piromalli] was in Armenia, he found Oskan *vardapet* and discussed with him the question of revising the Bible. The two compared [with the Vulgate] and made changes that disturbed the fluency of the original and altered the meanings.' Passages where Oskan's text agrees with the Latin Vulgate against all known Armenian manuscripts includes Matthew XVI:2–3 and XXIII:14; John VIII: 1–11; Acts XV:34, XXIII:24 and XXVIII:25, and, most significant of all, I John V:7. Below are cited three readings which show how Oskan tried to correct the Armenian text by using the Latin Vulgate based on the Hebrew. The additions from the Vulgate are placed in [ ] brackets.

(1) Exodus XVIII:12–13 '...et columnae decem [basesque totidem in ea quoque atrii latitudine, quae respicit ad orientem, quinquaginta cubiti erunt]...'
(2) Psalm XIII 3 'Omnes declinaverunt, simul inutiles facti sunt: non est qui faciat bonum,non est usque ad unum. [Sepulchrum patens est guttur eorum: linguis suis dolose agebant, venenum aspidum sub labiis eorum. Quorum os maledictione et amaritudine plenum est: veloces pedes eorum ad effundendum sanguinem. Contritio et infelicitas in viis eorum, et viam pacis non cognoverunt: non est timor Dei ante oculos eorum]. Nonne cognoscent omnes qui...'
(3) Isaiah XLV:4–6 '... et non cognovisti me. Ego Dominus, et non est amplius [extra me non est Deus: accinxi te, et non cognovisti me. Ut sciant hi, qui ab ortu solis, et qui ab occidente, quoniam absque me non est]. Ego Dominus, et non est alter.
(Oskan p. 84, 11–32, 224 cf.Biblia Sacra Vulgatae editionis, Romae, 1861, p. 343, 473).

Oskan Erevantsi included in the Old Testament the following forty-seven books arranged thus: 1. Genesis, 2. Exodus, 3. Leviticus, 4. Numbers, 5. Deuteronomy, 6. Joshua, 7. Judges, 8. Ruth, 9–12. Kingdoms I–IV,

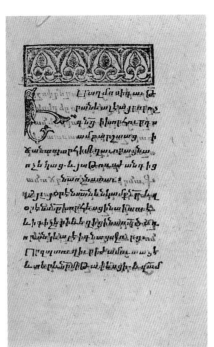

11 FAR LEFT Choirboys chanting the Psalms from the psalter printed by Abgar *dpir* Tokhatetsi in Venice, 1566. The initial 'B' in the bottom right corner of the picture correspond with the illustrations in the 1471 edition of the Malermi Bible. *The British Library, Or.70.a.9.*

12 LEFT Opening page of the only known copy of the psalter printed by Khatchatur Kesaratsi in the Monastery of All Saviour's in New Julfa, 1636–38. The press was the first in Persia and western Asia. *The Bodleian Library, Oxford, Vet.Or.f.Arm.I.*

13 BELOW The colophon at the beginning of the 'Letter to the Reader' from the psalter printed by Yovhannes Jughayetsi in Livorno, 1644. *The British Library, 218.a.32.*

13–14. Chronicles I–II, 15–16. Ezra I–II, 17. Nehemiah (= Ezra III), 18. Tobit, 19. Judith, 20. Esther, 21–22. Maccabees I–II, 23. Job, 24. Psalms, 25. Proverbs, 26. Ecclesiastes, 27. Song of Songs, 28. Wisdom of Solomon, 29. Wisdom of Sirach, 30. Isaiah, 31. Jeremiah, 32. Lamentations, 33. Baruch, 34. Ezekiel, 35. Daniel, 36. Hosea, 37. Joel, 38. Amos, 39. Obadiah, 40. Jonah, 41. Micah, 42. Nahum, 43. Habakkakuk, 44. Zephaniah, 45. Haggai, 46. Zachariah, 47. Malachi.

Of these 1–14, 16–17, 20, 23–27, 30–32 and 34–47 form part of the Hebrew canon and are regarded as canonical. Numbers 18–19, 21–22, 28–29 and 33 are from the Septuagint and are considered deutere-canonical. I Ezra is classed as non-canonical. The New Testament consists of twenty-seven books, of which II Peter, II John, III John and Revelation are regarded deutere-canonical. In the Oskanian Bible the New Testament books are followed by the Prayer of Manasseh and IV Ezra, which belong to the Old Testament. The six deutere-canonical books of the Old Testament are all present in Armenian manuscripts, and this gave Oskan Erevantsi the authority to include them in his printed edition of the Bible.

At the beginning of his edition he placed a eulogy in praise of Catholicos Hakob IV Jughayetsi (1598–1680), his mentor and sponsor. He also translated and included in his edition the prefaces and introductions of St Jerome to the books of the Bible. The book ends with a colophon 'To the Reader'.

The second half of the Oskanian Bible consists of 834 pages. In the Bodleian Library at Oxford there is a variant which has 808 pages, because the two apocryphal books not found in the Armenian canon – Prayers of Manasseh and IV Ezra – are excluded, reducing the book by twenty-six pages. In the first variant the Prayer of Manasseh and IV Ezra occupy pages 719–44, while in the second variant, although the pagination remains the same, the facing page has 'The Preface of Jerome'. During the printing of the first variant, Oskan was fully aware that these two books were apocryphal and excluded from the Armenian canon, to which he alludes in his introduction, but he included these two books in order to pass the Catholic censor. Eager to print a version of the Bible as close to the Armenian canon as

possible for his Armenian readers, he carefully retained all the features of the first printing but removed the Prayer of Manasseh and IV Ezra, adjusting the pagination in the Armenian alphabet and Arabic numbering. A second variant ending on page 808 instead of 834 was printed secretly to send to Armenia to escape the accusation of being called 'latinophile'. The assessment of Hovhannes Zohrabian (see below) that Oskan's handling of the text was 'reckless' is unwarranted.

The Armenian Bible has had these complete editions:

Amsterdam, 1666, Oskan Erevantsi
Constantinople, 1705, reprint of the 1666 edition
Venice, 1733, Mkhit'ar Sebastatsi's edition (a reprint of Oskan's edition with minor revisions)
Venice, 1805, Hovhannes Zohrabian
St Petersburg, 1817, reprint of the 1733 edition
Serampore, 1817, reprint of the 1733 edition
Venice, 1860, Arsen Bagratuni edition
Constantinople, 1892, American Bible Society edition (first five books of the Bible)
Constantinople, 1895, American Bible Society
Vienna, 1929, reprint of the Constantinople 1895 edition
Erevan, 1997, reprint of the Vienna 1929 edition

The second edition of the Bible in classical Armenian was prepared by Hovhannes Zohrabian (1758–1829), a member of the Catholic Order of the Mkhit'arist Congregation founded by Mkhit'ar Sebastatsi in 1715. It was published in 1805 in both single-volume and four-volume formats. In an extensive introduction, Zohrabian surveys the history of the Bible, explains his motivation for preparing a new edition and the reasons for his choice of manuscripts. These included seven complete Bibles mss. Nos 1508 (1319 AD), 1634 (1641 AD), 1006 (13–14th C.), 623, 229, Erevan 188, 1182, 1258 and Erevan 180, dating from 1295 to 1655. As a base manuscript for collation, Zohrabian chose Venice MS 1508, dated 1319. Of Cilician provenance, it belongs to Gevorg Skevratsi's recension and includes all the variant readings as notes without specifically indicating from which manuscript they come. His method of noting variants is not adequate to pinpoint their exact location. This is an indication that he was not attempting to estab-

14 The title-page of the first critical edition of the Bible printed by Hovhannes Zohrabian (1758–1829) on the Mkhit'arist press at Venice, St Lazzaro, 1805. *The British Library, Or.72.c.4.*

15 The title-page of the Bible printed by Arsen Bagratuni (Antimosian, 1766–1866) on the Mkhit'arist press, Venice, St Lazzaro, 1860. *Private collection.*

lish a critical text. For the Gospels he employed thirty manuscripts, and for the Acts and the Epistles forty manuscripts. These do not represent the whole corpus of manuscripts, and they exclude most of the very early testimonies. The honour of attempting to produce a single critical edition of the Bible by selecting and incorporating the 'pure' readings belongs to Arsen Bagratuni, who produced a partially successful edition in 1860. This publication, along with Zohrabian's, soon put the Oskanian edition out of circulation.

The Armenian Bible in the Modern Vernacular

In the mid-nineteenth century one of the decisive features of Armenian literature was the replacement of classical Armenian with the vernacular. The evolution of the vulgar or vernacular, which had first made its appearance in the fourteenth century, grew in stature to become the written language called *ashkharhabar* (secular dialect) in contrast to *grabar* (language of the book). In the second stage of its development, the vernacular split into two literary variants, eastern and western, based on the dialects of Erevan and Constantinople respectively. The triumph of liberalism in Europe in 1848, the growth and progress of Armenian printing, the national school system, and the secularization of Armenian language and literature brought into reality the prophecy of Grigor Ardsruni, founder of the famous daily *Mshak* (*Labourer*, 1872–1921): 'Yesterday we were an ecclesiastical community; tomorrow we shall be a nation of workers and thinkers.'

In 1818 William G. Goodell of Andover Theological Seminary in Boston, Massachusetts, published a report in the *Boston Recorder* entitled 'Brief History and State of Armenia as a Mission Field'. The Armenian people's reverence for the Bible, coupled with the tenacity of their Christian faith, were characteristics stressed in Goodell's report. Stating that the Armenian scriptures had been translated from the Syriac and Greek in the fifth century, he observed that 'had this translation descended to us unadulterated, its antiquity would have stamped upon it an inestimable value'. Unfortunately, the Armenian had become subjected to Roman Catholic influences over the years: the thirteenth-century Armenian King Het'um 'not only became a vassal of the Pope and a Franciscan monk', but also issued a new edition of the Armenian Bible that included 'all Jerome's prefaces and many alterations and corruptions from the Vulgate'. Should 'the pure and undefiled religion be revived in this Church', Goodell concluded, the Armenians, with their devotion to Christianity and their widely scattered commercial contacts throughout the Near East and Asia, could become a catalyst for the spread of Christianity. 'Give them the incorruptible seed, the word of God,' urged Goodell, 'and they will transport it with their other commodities to every country.'

William Goodell was clearly echoing the views of the English missionary Claudius Buchanan, rector of the College of Fort William in India. Impressed by the fact that the Armenians had established more churches in India than the ruling British had, Buchanan advocated the publication of the Armenian Bible both to meet the demand among the Armenians and to stimulate them into spreading the knowledge of the Gospel to other peoples; in this way the Armenian Bible would 'provide a right and precious fountain for the evangelization of the East'. Both Goodell and Buchanan stressed the devotion of the Armenians to the Bible, and both looked upon the Armenians not as a focus for Christian missions, but rather as assistants in the crusade to propagate the Christian faith throughout the world.

The missionary work of the Americans in the Near East was facilitated by the British and Foreign Bible Society (BFBS), which since 1804 had been pioneering the printing and distribution of Bibles throughout the world. Using the 1733 edition of the Bible prepared by Mkhit'ar Sebastatsi, it sponsored the publication of several editions in India (1819), St Petersburg (1817) and Constantinople (1823). Realizing, however, that the classical Armenian Bible could not be readily understood by the vast majority of Armenians, the BFBS supported the publication in St Petersburg of the New Testament in Armeno-Turkish in 1819, and commissioned Hovhannes Zohrabian, who had now moved to Paris, to prepare a version of the New Testament in modern Western vernacular. In 1824 the BFBS issued Zohrabian's modern Western Armenian New Testament, after revision by the Armenian scholar J. St Martin, in a bilingual format with the classical Armenian text. Zohrabian, who in his 1805 edition of the Bible had called Oskan's translations of Sirach and IV Ezra 'barbarous Armenian', also suffered criticism of his translation. BFBS agent Benjamin Baker described the style as 'too low... but...instead of the work being faulty, it is commendable on that account, as the women and less-instructed portion of the Armenian nation will be able to understand it'. Zohrabian was also commissioned to translate the Old Testament, but died in 1829 before being able to complete the project.

According to H.D. Leeves, the Society's agent in Constantinople, between the years 1822 and 1826 a total of 21,000 Bibles had been distributed in Constantinople, of which 10,531 had been distributed among Armenians, 6,595 among the Greeks, 1,916 among the Jews, and the remaining 2,000 copies in various European and Oriental languages. The BFBS insisted that the Bible be presented in its pure form, without notes or commentary. The Americans, on the other hand, considered the classical Greek text as the definitive version of the New Testament and the Hebrew as the definitive version of the Old Testament. They did not approve of the translation or publication of the Bible based on the classical Armenian. This was less of a problem with the Armenian New Testament, as it was close to the Greek; the Armenian Old Testament, however, based on the Septuagint, met with the missionaries' strong disapproval and they insisted that it be re-translated directly from the Hebrew.

The linguistic obstacles facing the American Missionaries in the Middle East were well understood by Goodell when he reported that the average person in the Middle East:

'...knows not what he prays, the prayers being always in an unknown tongue. Those at Constantinople, who pray in Arabic, speak only Turkish. The Maronites of Mount Lebanon, who speak Arabic, always pray in Syriac...the Greeks pray in ancient Greek, the Armenians in ancient Armenian, the Jews in Hebrew, the Catholics in Latin, and the few Christians found in Egypt in Coptic – all of which to them are dead languages. Whenever they have any business...they are careful to speak in a language which they understand. But whenever they have any business with their maker about their eternal interests, it is always done in a language which they understand not.'

In selecting a vernacular language for use by the Armenians, Goodell chose Armeno-Turkish, which is Turkish written in Armenian script and incomprehensible to those at whom it was aimed. Perhaps Goodell was anticipating the day when missionary work among the Muslims might be possible, for they were the only ones who could understand Armeno-Turkish. More likely, it was a practical decision, for while the Ottoman government forbade the import or circulation of the Bible in Turkish written in Arabic script, it did not prohibit Armeno-Turkish or Graeco-Turkish translations (Turkish in Armenian script). A final advantage was that the Armenian ecclesiastical authorities, although uneasy about the translation of the sacred Bible into Armenian, were less likely to oppose publications issued in Armeno-Turkish. Indeed, the Armenian Catholicos in Ējmiadsin had endorsed the Armeno-Turkish New Testament published in St Petersburg, and the Armenian Patriarch of Constantinople had even cooperated with the BFBS by recommending a translator and editor for a revised edition of the New Testament in that language. This seems particularly odd when the patriarchate refused permission to print the New Testament in Armenian in 1823, and said that if such a work was attempted, they 'would prohibit the perusal of it, and even punish such as should be found with it in their possession'. The American missionaries who followed William Goodell to Armenia in the 1830s – Henry G.I. Dwight, John B. Adger and Cyrus Hamlin – learned and used the vernacular Armenian languages either instead of, or in addition to, Armeno-Turkish. At that time vernacular Armenian was not considered a literary language; only the classical language had that status. Hamlin, the founder of a Mission High School on the Bosphorus in 1840, wrote that 'the idea of translating the Bible into [a vernacular] language was ridiculed. There was a very imperfect translation of the New Testament, and it was referred to with contempt...When the Bible and Bible teaching enter, the language takes on new meaning, grows with spiritual and moral forces...Modern Armenian is now wholly transformed; it has become a beautiful and cultivated language.'

The American who first gave serious study to the Armenian Bible was John B. Adger, who in 1834 assumed responsibility for Armenian-language printing at the missionary press, which had been moved in 1833 from Malta to Smyrna. Adger was asked by the American Bible Society to prepare a new version of the New Testament in classical and modern Armenian. It was said that the Zohrabian New Testament was deficient both in the modern vernacular Armenian and also because it was based on the classical Armenian text. Adger was immediately and favourably impressed by the classical Armenian text and the skill of the fifth-century tranlsators. Writing to his superiors, he offered the following assessment:

'If possible, I would wish to avoid the necessity of giving offence to the nation by altering their old version, a version for which they entertain feelings of the deepest veneration, and one which well deserves their esteem... Excepting some interpolations by subsequent copyists, none of which however are of a serious nature, the version is truly admirable. I do not believe it is at all inferior...to our own excellent English translation.'

In comparing the Armenian with the Greek text, Adger claimed that the differences were slight and of no more importance than similar cases in English. Adger argued that 'if the good people in America cannot bear to have Dr Webster [a lexicographer] alter any words or phrases in our revered translation, how can we expect that the Armenians will tolerate an analogous attempt, by strangers, whose orthodoxy they so much suspect?'

Adger's arguments won the day and he completed his edition of the New Testament in classical Armenian with the Greek variants printed in Armenian in the margins. The Gospels, printed in Smyrna in 1837, were the first to appear, followed by the whole New Testament in 1838. Working with a number of Armenian assistants, Adger then revised the Zohrabian translation of the New Testament into modern Western Armenian, publishing the four Gospels in 1841 and the entire New Testament in 1842. The Armenian-language printing of the Bible took on a new importance when the Armenian Protestant Community was formed in 1850, and hired the linguist and scholar Elias Riggs to prepare new editions. In 1853 the Smyrna press printed the complete Bible in modern Armenian.

Commentaries on the Books of the Bible

St John Chrysostom repeatedly bids his hearers read the Bible for themselves: 'Hear, I adjure you, all secular folk, get yourselves the Bibles, which are medicine for the soul; or at least, if you will do no more, get yourselves the New Testament.' Elsewhere he emphasizes Christ's command: 'Christ, referring the Jews to the scriptures, sent them not to a mere reading but to accurate examination. For He did not say [merely] read the scriptures, but search the scriptures... He commands them to dig with exactitude in order that they may find those things that lie deep.' Finally, he even insists upon the Bible as the ultimate touchstone of truth: 'For, even

as a safe door, so doth it shut out heretics from entrance, setting up in safety concerning all the things which we desire, and not permitting us to go astray.' Here, as early as the late fourth century, we have evidence that explains the different attitudes of the Eastern and Western churches in the Middle Ages towards the Bible.

Soon after inventing the Armenian alphabet in the 'wonderful land of Armenia', Moses, the prophets and Paul 'became Armenian-speaking'. The Armenian version of the Bible had a tremendous impact on the development of Armenian literature and the Armenian mind not only in the fifth century, but also in the succeeding centuries. Since Armenian literature began with the Bible, the Armenian historian Nicholas Adontz (1871–1942) summed up the impact of the Bible in these words: 'The Latin Vulgate did not have the same importance to the Latin countries as the Armenian Bible to the Armenian people. The Latin literature had been in existence for a long time when the Vulgate appeared, whereas the Armenian Bible inaugurated the beginnings of a new era in which the Armenian people, learning for the first time the use of the pen, came to take their place in the world of human civilization.' In the words of Koriwn: '...a land that had not known even the name of the regions where all those wonderful divine acts had been performed, soon learned all the things that were, not only those that had transpired in time, but that of the eternity which had preceded, and those that had come later, the beginning and the end and all the divine traditions'.

The place of sacred scripture in the intellectual life of medieval people is hard to overestimate. Beryl Smalley has described this situation in the West, where until the twelfth century the word 'theology' did not exist; the study of religion was simply called *sacra pagina* or *lectio divina*, meaning the study of sacred scriptures. A parallel situation pertained in the East a good deal longer, since a scholastic systematization of doctrine was never introduced there. In twelfth-century Constantinople the patriarchal school divided all theology among three Chairs of Exegesis: the Gospel, St Paul's Epistles and the Psalms. Christian doctrine was, in a sense, coterminous with the interpretation of sacred scripture.

Like other branches of Armenian literature, Armenian commentaries took their start from the series of translations made from Greek and Syriac in the fifth and sixth centuries by 'senior' and 'junior' translators. Among the early Church fathers, the following works were translated:

Genesis: Ephrem the Syrian, John Chrysostom
Octateuch: Eusebius of Emesa
Genesis to Chronicles: Ephrem
Job: Ephrem the Syrian, Hesychius
Psalms: Daniel the Syrian, Epiphanius, John
    Chrysostom, Theodoret
Song of Songs: Hippolytus, Origen

Isaiah: John Chrysostom
Ezekiel: Cyril of Alexandria
Diatessaron: Ephrem the Syrian
Matthew: John Chrysostom
John: John Chrysostom
Acts: Cyril of Alexandria, Ephrem the Syrian,
    John Chrysostom
Epistles: Ephrem the Syrian, John Chrysostom
Hebrew: Cyril of Alexandria
Apocalypse: Andrew and Aretas

The preference of the Armenians for the Antiochene theology was explained by the fact that the leading figures of that school were staunch upholders of the faith of

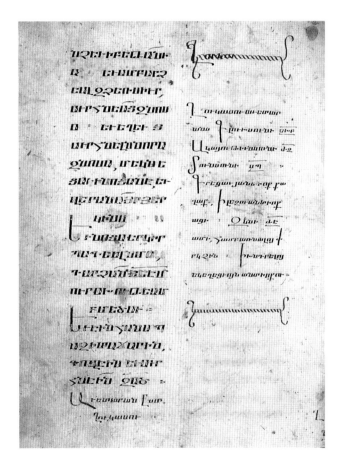

16 The four Gospels in square uncials of 1166. This folio (239v) placed at the end of St Luke's Gospel, records: 'Luke's Gospel has 342 chapters, 15 testimonies, 2,800 paragraphs. It was written in Antioch in the Antiochene tongue seventeen years after the Ascension of the Saviour. At the request of the Church of Antioch'.
The British Library, ms. 19, 727, f.239v.

Nicaea. In particular, John Chrysostom, the leading Antiochene scholar of that time, remained free of any suspicion of heretical taint. But the indigenous commentary tradition has its own frame of reference. It adopted elements of interpretation from various traditions of exegesis linking them together, creating what p'. Ant'apyan calls 'chain commentary' [catena]. In these commentaries we find passages from Antiochene and Alexandrian biblical scholars widely quoted.

The earliest original commentary belongs to the historian Eghishē, whose commentary on the books of Joshua, Judges and Genesis is often mentioned by Armenian writers, although the complete text was already lost in the thirteenth century (*c.* 1200–71). Extensive extracts from it have survived in the works of Vardan Areveltsi, and in several manuscripts which the academic Levon Khatchikyan assembled into a seminal work in 1945 and which was recently republished.

The subsequent history of Armenian biblical scholarship is associated with the monastic school in the province of Siwnik', where in the words of the historian Step'anos Orbelian (*c.* 1260–1304), the monks were 'versed in holy scriptures and were accomplished exegetes'. Famous representatives of the Siwnik' school from the sixth to the eighth century whose works have not been preserved include Petros Siwnetsi (d. 557), Mat'usghan (634–641), Movses bishop Siwnetsi (d. 725), and Step'anos Siwnetsi (d. 735). The literary heritage of the Siwnik monastery was lost in 1170, when the Seljuk army captured the fort at Baghaberd and burnt the 10,000 manuscripts held there.

The first exegete whose *Commentary on the Lectionary* has reached us is Grigoris Arsharuni (*c.* 650–*c.* 729). This was published in Constantinople in 1728 as an appendix to Cyril of Jerusalem's *Catechetical Lectures on Baptism*. According to the historian Step'anos Asoghik (*c.* 935–*c.* 1015), Grigoris participated in the Church Council of Manazkert, convened by Catholicos Yovhannes Odznetsi in 725, and put his signature to the proceedings. The first complete commentary to reach us from the Siwnik school is that of Step'anos Siwnetsi: *Commentary on the Four Gospels* was compiled by request of Catholicos Davit' I (728–741). The work, presumed lost, was rediscovered in 1917 by Archbishop Garegin Hovspeants (1867–1952) in a manuscript dated 1155

(Holy Ējmiadsin ms. No. 446, now Matenadaran 5551). Although submitted for publication in 1950, it was delayed by turmoil in the Antelias Catholicate. The work was eventually published in 1988 in Athens, and reprinted in Erevan in 1994. Step'anos Siwnetsi provides an interpretation of the 'difficult' passages in St Matthew's Gospel, making textual corrections and commenting on sections of the three other Gospels that have no parallels in Matthew.

Grigor Narekatsi (945–1003), one of the greatest Christian mystic poets of all time, composed a *Commentary on the Song of Songs* at the request of King Gurgen (968–1003). In the colophon of his work, Narekatsi states that he began the work in 977 at the behest of 'God-loving and Christ-crowned King Gurgen Ardsruni'. The Song of Songs is one piece of erotic literature in the Bible, which in later Jewish litugial tradition was allegorized as an account of God's love for Israel. This Jewish tradition was also adopted by Christian commentators, who clearly prefered to read the book symbolically rather than as a treatment of sexual and erotic love. Hence the dominant Christian interpretations of the Song have focused on the relationship between Christ and the Church or Christ and the individual soul. Grigor Narekatsi expounds on the holiness of marriage and praises love that binds man and woman. He also expressed the bold (for his time) idea that Eve was deceived and 'Adam, not wanting to separate from his wife, had eaten the fruit and for love's sake and not in order to become divine as Eve had desired'. This *Commentary* has had several printings and was reprinted in Venice in 1789 and 1877.

Anania Sanahntsi (d. 1070) composed a *Commentary on the Gospel of St Matthew* in the Monastery of Sanahin at the command of its abbot, Dioskoros (1037–63). Unfortunately, only the first ten chapters of the work survive in Matenadaran ms. No. 2688, copied in the twelfth century and ms. No. 2859 of the nineteenth century.

The poet Catholicos Nerses IV Klayetsi (1102–73), was a graduate of the Karmir Vank (Red Monastery) in Cilician Armenia where 'scholarly erudition and deep spiritual life were pursued, wholeheartedly devoted to the interpretation of the word of God and the spiritual values of the Christian faith'. Like all graduates of this

17 Grigor *vardapet* Khlatetsi (1349–1425), founder of the monastic school at Tsip'nay Monastery, teaching his pupils Psalm I:1, 'Blessed is the man'. From the Gospels of Grigor Khlatetsi, Tsip'nay Monastery, 1419.
Matenadaran, Erevan, ms. 3714, f.14v.

place, Klayetsi was awarded the honorific title of Shnorhali ('full of grace'). He composed his *Commentary on the Gospel of St Matthew* at the command of his brother Catholicos Grigor III Pahlavuni (1113–66) in the monastery of Hromklay, but he got only as far as Matthew V:17. The work was completed in the fourteenth century by Yovhannes Erznkatsi, called Dsord-soretsi, the exegete of Gladzor. The commentary was printed in Constantinople on 16 March 1825 using one manuscript. The work is of special significance, for it is prefaced with a *Commentary on the ten Canon Tables*. In an extended preface, Nerses IV Klayetsi explains the link between the Ten Commandments of Moses and the ten Canon Tables and their symbolism in Christian art. The colophon in the manuscript notes that the work of Nerses Shnorhali and Dsordsoretsi is regarded as a 'lighted lantern and bright beacon on top of a church tower, that enlightens all the believers of Christ'.

From Matthew V:18, 'For verily I say unto you, till heaven and earth pass...', Dsordsoretsi continued the commentary left incomplete by Shnorhali 'for the 'purpose of teaching the scriptures' to the monks and pupils. Aristakes and Ephrem, former pupils of Shnorhali, attempted to complete the unfinished commentary of their teacher by compiling the works of Epiphanus of Cyprus, Ephrem the Syrian, Cyril of Alexandria and John Chrysostom. The compilation has reached us in over thirty manuscripts.

Another graduate of the Karmir Monastery was Sargis Shnorhali (*c.* 1100–67), a contemporary of Nerses Shnorhali. He wrote a *Commentary on the Seven Catholic Epistles*, which was printed in Constantinople in 1826 by Andreas *vardapet* Narinian, using two choice manuscripts from St James's Armenian Patriarchate collections. Sargis Shnorhali is also attributed with a *Commentary on Isaiah*.

Another Cilician, Ignatios *vardapet* Sevleṙntsi (*c.* 1090–*c.* 1160), on the command of Catholicos Grigor III Pahlavuni, composed a *Commentary on the Gospel of St Luke*. According to the historian Kirakos Gandzaketsi, Ignatios refused to carry out the task at first, complaining of lack of expertise. Then he had a dream in which he saw a large group of Armenian *vardapets* sitting in front of a bright door. They bar him from entering for refusing to compile the commentary on the Gospel. Spurred by the dream, Ignatios wrote his commentary, which he described as being 'not of deep learning and not in the vernacular'. This commentary has had two printed editions, in 1735 and 1824, both in Constantinople, using a single manuscript. He is also credited with having written a *Commentary on the Acts of the Apostles*.

Sargis Kund (*c.* 1100–85) was among the exegetes to employ the compilation method to compose his *Commentary on the Gospel of Luke* in 1178. In the colophon of his work he listed his sources as being Ephrem the Syrian, Cyril of Alexandria, Step'anos Siwnetsi, John Chrysostom, Gregory the Theologian, Epiphanius of Cyprus, Gregory of Narek, Sargavag *vardapet*, Movses

K'ert'ogh and Mambrē *Verdsanogh*. In the thirteenth century, this work was used as textbook in the Monastery of Medsop'. It survives in three manuscripts, dated 1184, 1427 and 1821. Using the same method, Sargis Kund also compiled a commentary on the Gospel of St John. The work, based on the commentaries of Step'anos Siwnetsi, John Chrysostom and Ephrem the Syrian, is available in only two manuscripts dated 1644 and 1706.

Among thirteenth-century authors with multi-faceted talents, Vardan Areweltsi (*c.* 1200–71) is the leading figure. Born in Gandzak, he was the pupil of Vardan *Vanakan* and a contemporary of Kirakos Areweltsi. In 1240 he went on a pilgrimage to Jerusalem and on his way back passed through Cilicia, where he remained between 1241 and 1251, acting as counsellor to Catholicos Kostandin Bardzrberdtsi and King Het'um I. In 1251 he returned to eastern Armenia and taught in various major monastic institutions, among them Andrei, Kayenaberd, Haghpat and Khor Virap. p'. Ant'apyan in his noteworthy research on Vardan Areweltsi lists the following commentaries:

(1) *Commentary on the Pentateuch*, which he wrote in the monastery of Khor Virap in 1261 at the behest of Archbishop Hamazasp, abbot of the monastery of Haghpat. This voluminous work is better known under the title of *Commentary on Genesis*. Abridged by Grigor *vardapet* Khlatetsi in 1418 as *Abbreviated Commentary on the Books of the Creation Compiled from the Writings of Vardan Vardapet* (Mat. ms. No. 5574), it draws on the commentaries of Ephrem the Syrian, Gregory of Nyssa, Cyril of Alexandria, John Chrysostom, Eghishē, Philo and others.

(2) *Commentary on the Psalms of David*, published in Astrakhan in 1797, appeared under the incorrect name, Vardan Bardzberdtsi. The colophon of a *Calendar of Feasts*, copied by Aveweltsi's pupil Tiratsu in 1267, attributes the commentary to Vardan Areweltsi. In the title of the work in ms. No. 5163 the author Vardan Areweltsi records that the work was written on the request of Jovhannes, abbot of the monastery of Haghpat, between 1245 and 1257, drawing on the works of Athanasius, Epiphanius, Ephrem the Syrian and Nerses Lambronatsi. It is

important to note that, according to the author, the commentary was intended for 'teaching the youth of Sion', a claim confirmed by Grigor Tat'evatsi in his own commentary, where he acknowledges his debt to Vardan Areweltsi.

(3) *Commentary on the Song of Songs.* The authorship of this work is in no doubt. The title in ms. No. 1144 states that Areweltsi wrote the work in 1255 at the request of his compatriot Kirakos (Gandzaketsi) based on the works of Gregory of Nyssa, Origen, Hippolytus and Gregory of Narek.

(4) *Commentary on the Book of Daniel.* Areweltsi wrote this work in the monastery of Khor Virap between 1267 and 1268, as he states in the colophon of ms. No. 5452. He quotes extensively from the works of Hippolytus, Ephrem and Stepanos Siwnetsi. The work was printed by Andreas *vardapet* Narinian in Nerses Lambronatsi's *Commentary on the Twelve Minor Prophets* in Constantinople, 1825.

(5) *Commentary on Ezekiel.* This is a comparatively small work.

The most brilliant yet often controversial author of the twelfth century was Nerses Lambronatsi (1153–98) the grandson of Nerses Shnorhali's brother. A graduate of the monasteries of Skevra and Hromklay, he was well versed in Greek, Latin, Hebrew and Syriac, and wrote his *Commentary on the Armenian Liturgy* at the young age of twenty-four. He also wrote commentaries on several books of the Bible – Genesis, Proverbs, the Wisdom of Solomon, the Song of Songs, the Twelve Minor Prophets, Psalms, Daniel, the Gospels of St Matthew, the Catholic Epistles, and the Revelation of John.

Lambronatsi's *Commentary on the Twelve Minor Prophets* was printed in Constantinople in 1825, using 'three choice manuscripts' from the library of Hovhannes Kolot (1678–1741), Armenian Patriarch of Constantinople. Lambronatsi's translation of the Revelation of John passed into the Armenian canon, and he also translated a sixth-century commentary on the Revelation of John by Andreas of Caesarea, which was printed in Jerusalem in 1855. For the publication of this text, three manuscripts were used, the earliest of which was a manuscript copied in Karin in 1306. Lambronatsi acquired the Greek manuscript in Antioch and took it to Hromklay,

where Catholicos Gregory IV (1137–97) gave it to the Greek metropolitan Kostand to render into Armenian. Nerses Lambronatsi copied the translation in his own hand in 1179, and attached two colophons to it. In the first colophon he argues the case for the canonical status of Revelation, quoting evidence from Dionysius the Areopagite, Irenaeus of Lyons, Gregory of Nazianzus, Gregory of Nyssa, Cyril of Alexandria, Origen and others on the basis of which 'Revelation was placed among the canon of the New Testament'. In the second colophon he gives an account of how he found the manuscript and presented it to Catholicos Gregory IV, and which was then translated into Armenian in 1179 in the Holy and Patriarchal See of Hromklay. This is an important testimony for deciding the acceptance date of the Revelation of St John into the Armenian canon.

The only known commentary on the Gospel of St Mark belongs to the monk Barsegh Mashkevortsi (d. 1345/50), which he composed in 1325 in the monastery of Mashkevor in Cilicia. Unfortunately, only part of the work (IX:11–XVI) has survived. It was published by Andreas Narinian in Constantinople in 1826, comparing two sixteenth- and seventeenth-century manuscripts. The work has survived in thirty-five manuscripts, one of which (ms. No. 1314) is the author's own manuscript written in 1325.

Gladzor, the other great centre of biblical learning in Siwnik', flourished for only sixty years, from 1280 to 1340, but left behind a rich intellectual heritage. Under the patronage of Prince Proshian, Gladzor grew rapidly into a proper university. Contemporary writers speak of it as 'the seat and school of our holy doctors', 'glorious second Athens', 'metropolis of all forms of learning' and 'celebrated holy monastery and university'. The leading teachers were Nerses Mshetsi (d. 1284), and his pupil Esayi *vardapet* Ntchetsi (*c.* 1255–1338), who composed a commentary on the Book of Ezekiel in 1303 at the request of Step'anos Orbelian, drawing from the works of John Chrysostom, Cyril of Alexandria, Ephrem the Syrian and Step'anos Siwnetsi. A pupil of his, Yovhannes Erznkatsi (*c.* 1260–*c.* 1335) is known to have copied a Gladzor manuscript in 1306, which contains three commentaries: *Commentary on the Gospel of John* by Step'anos Siwnetsi and Nana the Syrian, and *Commentary on the Revelation* attributed to John of Cappadocia

18 Archbishop Esayi
Ntchetsi (*c.* 1255–1338),
abbot of the University of
Gladzor, teaching. From
the *Commentary on Isaiah*
by Gevork' *vardapet*,
Skevra monastery,
Cilicia, 1299.
*St James's Monastery,
Jerusalem, ms. 365, f.2r.*

(Mat. No. 206). Jovhannes Erznkatsi's exegetical work, like that of Nerses Shnorhali, established a firm interrelation between text and pictures and their works are vital sources for artists working on illumination. Pictures and text in manuscripts often travel together over long stretches of time, so the process of copying one must have had a bearing on the other. Yovhannes Orotnetsi (1315–87), a pupil of Esayi Ntchetsi, left Gladzor and joined the famous monastery at Tat'ev, where he wrote commentaries on the Gospels of St Matthew and St John, the Epistles of Paul, III Paul to the Corinthians, and Isaiah. His pupil Grigor Tat'evatsi (1344–1409), renowned philosopher and polemicist, was a prolific author, whose works include *Commentaries on Isaiah* (1384), the *Psalms* (1405), *Proverbs*, the *Wisdom of Solomon* and the *Song of Songs* (1405), and the *Gospels of St John* and *St Matthew* (1409). None of these have been printed except a short version of the *Commentary on the Psalms* which was published in 1993 by Armine K'yoshkeryan using ms. No. 1131 of the Matenadaran, which is the earliest and the most reliable. In the Biblical Commentaries series recently initiated to mark the 1700th anniversary of the declaration of Christianity in Armenia, the commentary on the Proverbs by Hamam Areweltsi (825–90) was published using ms. No. 1138 of the St James Armenian Patriarchate prepared by Mkhitar Saribekyan.

The Bible in Armenian Literature

The work of the translators, which began with the invention of the Armenian alphabet and concluded with the translation of the Bible into classical Armenian, is memorably summarized in the words of the hymn sung on the feast day of the translators: 'Who by divine dispensation decorated the meaning of the Only Begotten by creating living letters, to lead the flock of the new Israel'. The translation of the Bible opened the path towards an exceptional cultural ferment. In a short space of time, according to Koriwn, Mesrop 'separated and purged them [the Armenians] from their native traditions and made them forget to such an extent that they said "I forgot my people and my father's house"'.

The stamp of the Bible on Armenian historiography is explicit. Professor Robert W. Thomson, an American academic who has published English translations of the Armenian historians Agat'angeghos (1976), Movses Khorenatsi (1978), Eghishē (1982), T'ovma Ardsruni (1985), Ghazar P'arpetsi (1991) and Sebeos (1999), acknowledges that 'the Bible was the literary resource *par excellence*, and themes from the Old and New Testaments constantly appear. Indeed, biblical vocabulary is so pervasive that it is often difficult to decide whether a parallel is being hinted at, or whether the historian naturally expressed himself in such a fashion with no further nuance intended.' For example, the claim in Genesis (VIII: 4) that the ark rested upon the mountains of Ararat served as a source for the fifth-century historian P'awstos Buzand to create the legend, adding 'the mountains of Armenia to mount Sararad' (III: 10). In a similar act of embellishment the fifth-century historian Movses Khorenatsi made Togarmah (Genesis X: 3) the father of Hayk, founder of the Armenian nation (I: 5).

According to Professor Thomson the Bible offered a model for the writing of history in a Christian context – 'that is, a model for the description of the working of God's providence in the present world'. Several Armenian historians regarded the writing of history as a demonstration of the ultimate triumph of piety and truth over the forces of evil and death.

The Bible has also had a profound impact on Armenian religious poetry and on *sharakan* (hymns) in particular. Mesrop Mashtots, who wrote the hymns sung during Lent, was inspired by episodes from the Bible:

'Father, compassionate, I confess to thee, like the prodigal son, forgive my sins and have mercy'

'Lord, who had mercy on the woman from Cana, have mercy on me, the sinner, and forgive'

'Lord, who converted the tax-collector to the wisdom of light, convert me also the lost and have mercy'.

The best religious poetry in classical Armenian is *The Lamentations* of Gregory of Narek (945–1003), which has left a longlasting impact on all subsequent religious poetry in Armenian. In ninety poems, which he describes as 'mystic soliloquies with God', Gregory of Narek seeks union with Jesus, and ultimately with God the Father, since God, Jesus and the Holy Spirit form the Trinity. Therefore he asks Jesus:

'And by thine hand willingly it [Holy Spirit] offereth
 me pure,
Being itself mighty, presenteth me unto the Father,
That once near him, with him, ever in thee,
Wholly bound with my breath with thy grace,
I may write with thee inseparably.'

In so doing, he achieves immortality in this world, so he entreats the Lord:

'Accept the woven fabric of these heart-rending sobs
And smell this verbal gift
As a bloodless sacrifice.
Confirm it, certify it, affix your seal to it
As eternal sculpture
Along with other select and pleasing works.'

Long before John Milton's *Paradise Lost* (1667), there was a tradition of rewriting parts of the Bible in verse, a tradition often traced back to the hexaemeron literature of the patristic commentaries which dealt with the account of the creation of the universe in six days, as set forth in Genesis I. Gregory Magistros (990–1059) is the author of the epic *Hazartoghean* (One Thousand Lines) in which he summarizes the story of the Bible in verse. In the preface of the work, published in Venice 1868,

19 St Gregory of Narek (945–1003) offering his *Book of Lamentations* as 'verbal gift' to Christ. From a manuscript by the artist Grigor Mlitshetsi copied for Archbishop Nerses Lambronatsi (1153–98), Skevra monastery, Cilicia, 1179.
Matenadaran, Erevan, ms. 1568, f.177v.

Magistros confides to the reader that while he was in Constantinople in 1045, he made the acquaintance of Manutche, a learned Arab poet. Manutche maintained that the Koran was superior to the Bible because it was written in verse (mono-rhymed). Magistros responded that whereas Muhammad had taken forty years to write the Koran, he could put the Bible into verse in four days. Manutche, considering the feat impossible, offered to become a Christian if Magistros succeeded. As promised, Magistros composed a resumé of the Bible in 1016 lines, declaring that 'the Holy Spirit comes to strengthen

20 A portrait of Nerses IV Klayetsi (Nerses Shnorhali) the poet, theologian and Catholicos of All Armenians (1166–73), at prayer in front of an altar. This illustration comes from a breviary illuminated by the artist Step'annos Vahkatsi, Cilicia, *c.* fourteenth century. *The British Library, ms. Or.13993, f.1r.*

past and the Armenian present. Nerses Shnorhali, the grandson of Grigor Magistros, wrote a 1500-line poem called *Ban Hawatoy* in 1152. An apologia for church doctrine, it put into verse the Gospel of St John, in thirty-six verses that correspond to the thirty-six letters of the Armenian alphabet. It was expanded into an epic poem of 2000 mono-rhymed couplets in three books: the Old Testament representing human past history; the New Testament representing the present; and the Last Judgement representing the future of human history. The work is called *Yisus Ordi* (Jesus the Only Begotten Son), which the author describes as a 'conversation with God', recalling biblical events and scenes, each of which has a personal application for the reader, and providing occasions for meditation and prayers.

'From Salem, our Paradise,
With Adam the sinner,
Did I descend to the lower Jericho,
To fall into the hands of thieves,
Who both stripped me of the Light
And filled my soul with the wounds of sin,
And departed, leaving me not half
But quite dead from the encounter.'

'Behold, within me there is set
A city built by thine own hand.
Intelligence Thou gavest me
To judge my widowed soul.'

'Teach me to judge with righteousness
My soul and mind, so that I be
Not cast in prison till I pay
The last farthing which they demand.'

Nerses Shnorhali insisted on verse as his preferred mode of expression, despite criticism. Citing the Psalms and the Song of Songs in the Bible as justification for writing about a sacred subject in verse, he insisted that for teaching purposes, reading poetry was a more pleasurable experience. To add to its effectiveness, sections of 'Jesus the Son' were put to music and sung. In a manuscript of Canticles (ms. No. 2672), several have the instruction: 'If you do not know the mode, sing it in the mode of *Yisus Ordi.*' This is evidence that the poem was recited in

us and He teaches us the whole truth'. Thereupon, Manutche 'confessed with fear and trembling that the God of the Christians is great'. The 1016 lines of the epic divide into three sections: lines 1–353 cover the Old Testament, lines 354–891 the New Testament, and lines 892–1016 cover in more sentimental terms the spread of Christianity and the conversion of the Armenian people, ending with a personal prayer by the author. His reworking of the biblical tradition may well be described as a mythopoetic revision rooted in a particular view of salvation history that saw continuity between the biblical the same syle as the national epic poem *Sasuntsi David*. After the Bible and the *Book of Lamentations (Narek)* of Grigor Narekatsi, 'Jesus the Son' was the most widely read book among the Armenians, with as many as twelve editions between 1643 and 1830.

Another poet, Yovhannes Tlkurantsi (1489–1525), wrote 'On the Creation of the World', which, according to Norayr Pogharian, is a verse abridgment of Vardan's *Commentary on Genesis* (see page 42). Making use of the Bible, Tlkurantsi retells the story of Creation, weaving into the biblical text various stories and traditions to make a rich poetic narrative.

Finally the most original re-working of the Bible belongs to the poet Aṙak'el Siwnetsi (1350–1431), nephew of the great exegete and philosopher Grigor Tat'evatsi. Siwnetsi has a distinctive place in Armenian literature as the author of two poems: *Drakhtagirk* (Paradise Book) and *Adamgirk* (Adam Book)

Drakhtagirk is an interesting literary conception. It describes human life in heaven and hell, where human beings are confined to live according to the merits of their life on earth; eternal happiness for the just, and torment and torture for the sinners. The hero of the poem, who is the author himself, accompanies the reader to hell, where the inhabitants advise the visitors to live a good and sin-free life in order to be rewarded with blessed life in the eternal kingdom.

Adamgirk, a dramatic poem composed in 1401, has had three versions. It comprises 1740 lines reworking the story of Adam and Eve and the loss of paradise. The central theme is taken from Genesis, enriched with legends and folklore from Apocryphal literature, and draws on the literary legacies of Grigor Narekatsi and Nerses Shnorhali. Critics have compared it to Dante Alighieri's *Divine Comedy (c.* 1307) and John Milton's *Paradise Lost* (1667). *Adamgirk* has appeared in four editions: 1721 and 1799 in Constantinople, 1907 in Venice and 1989 in Erevan.

The Bible and the Scribe

'In times of war and invasion carry the manuscripts to the cities and bury them, but in times of peace take them out and read them, for closed books are like idols.'

'Of what use are my creations when my sight has failed? But nurse the hope, at least, they'll be of use to coming generations.' (Matenadaran ms. No. 1418, 1280 AD).

Armenian Christian culture begins with the Bible, and the first text written with the new alphabet was 'to know wisdom and instruction; to perceive the words of understanding'. The historian Ghazar P'arpetsi testifies that soon after Sahak had brought the great spiritual labour of translating the Bible to completion, 'schools were immediately established for the instruction of the flock and the ranks of scribes were increased, and they emulated each other'. He continues,

'the services of the holy church were embellished. Crowds of men and women in the congregation were stimulated at the festivals of the Saviour and the commemorations of the martyrs. Old and young, succoured and filled with spiritual profit, ran joyfully from participation in the great mystery [liturgy] back to each one's house, singing psalms and antiphons everywhere, in the squares and streets and at home. The churches were rendered glorious; the martyria of the saints received lustre, continually embellished by testaments and gifts. Torrents were continuously flowing from the commentators, who explained the secrets of the prophets and placed before all the people tables loaded with spiritual dishes...the land of Armenia was filled with the knowledge of the Lord.'

Two elements in this testimony are important: (a) 'the ranks of scribes were increased' and (b) 'the martyria of the saints received manuscripts of Testaments' [ukht ktakaranats]. P'arpetsi's account confirms that soon after the invention of the Armenian alphabet, scriptoriums were founded in holy Ējmiadsin, where scribes copied manuscripts of the testaments which were then presented to the martyriums set up in memory of the saints.

The manuscript has traditionally been the Armenian religious object *par excellence*, comparable to the reliquary in the Western Catholicism and the icon in the Greek Orthodox Church. Armenian manuscripts were the locus of faith, to be treasured and guarded. Just as the Byzantine emperors sometimes carried an icon as a talisman during their military campaigns, the Armenians took with them the Holy Gospel. Manuscripts attributed with miraculous powers were given special names, such as 'Saviour of All', or 'Resurrector of the Dead', just as special names were given to particular icons. The 20,000-plus manuscripts that have survived, more than any other ancient version, with the exception only of the Latin Vulgate, testify to the important place they occupied in the lives of the people. The manuscripts were thought of as pledges to ensure the salvation of the sponsors, as imperishable treasures that would guarantee a place in heaven. This also explains why Armenian manuscripts are rarely anonymous productions. The sponsors, as well as the scribes and the painters, wished to record their participation in this pious act so that they might be recalled in the prayers of all those who had occasion to use these manuscripts. From very early on the act of sponsoring a manuscript or receiving one was considered a religious imperative. In the words of Christ: 'Lay not up for yourself treasures upon earth, where moth and rust doth corrupt, and where thieves break through and steal: but lay up for yourself treasures in heaven, where neither moth nor rust doth corrupt; and where thieves do not break through nor steal' (Matthew VI: 19–20). This understanding is beautifully expressed by a scribe in a colophon of a Gospel copied in 1620: 'The ways of doing good and nearing God are many, the greatest being martyrdom, then by the life of monasticism and

21 Virgin and Child, with the expensively robed kneeling figure of Chancellor Hanēs of King Levon. An inscription in white uncials above him reads: 'Mother of God, Baron Hanēs, Chancellor, prayers to thee in his soul'. From a Psalter by Sargis Pidsak, Cilicia, fourteenth century.
The British Library, ms. Or.13804, f.2v.

finally by purchasing books of the scriptures for the glory of God, to aid personal salvation and benefit the public.' The recurrent theme in the colophons is the hope that future readers of the manuscripts would not fail to remember and pray for the sponsor, the scribe, the binder, or the restorer. In many a colophon the sponsor says that he acquired the manuscript as an 'indelible memorial or monument' to his own soul and to those of his immediate family, as well as his relatives, both living and deceased, many of whom are mentioned by name. The colophon of a royal Psalter copied for King Levon II (1269–89) by the scribe Yohan and illuminated by Sargis Pidsak reads: 'Falling in love with this all-embracing treasure-house of good things, the pious and godly king of the Armenians, King Levon, heir and inheritor of the crown of this kingdom of the Armenian people...at whose command this psalter of David was written for the embellishment of the church and for the instruction of the children of New Zion, and having his own wish to sing and psalm and speak with God at his leisure and to remain mindful of his good things in future time.'

Frequently, manuscripts were copied or sponsored because the individual recalled the words, 'Blessed is he who has a child in Zion', and many received a manuscript 'as a child in Zion and as an intimate friend in Jerusalem' (Mat. ms. 4083, 1331 AD), the 'child in Zion' being the manuscript itself. Through its colophon – called *yishatakaran*, literally 'place of memory' – the manuscript carries on the name of its owner, and allies him with the saving powers of the Armenian Church. A manuscript of the four Gospels copied by the scribe Gaspar Erets in Isfahan in 1686 at the request of the lady Eghisabeth pleads that the offering be 'a memory of her soul and those of his parents, having in mind the words of Isaiah, who says blessed is he who has child in Zion and family in Jerusalem, and in that hope the sponsor received this Gospel decorated with flowers in gold' (Calouste Gulbenkian Museum, ms. No. LA216).

Prince Het'um I (1213–70), who had a Gospel copied for him in 1293 in Cilicia, explains in the colophon why he wanted a Gospel manuscript to be written for the new church he had built in the fort of Korikos: 'In there and for the illumination of souls, the Gospel of Christ was necessary to be in the Eden of the church, as was the tree of life in the Garden of Eden.' Het'um, the great commander of the Armenian army, took three steps to protect his land and his people against the enemy. First he built a fortress on the island facing Korikos. Next he built a church in the new fortress, and finally, he 'planted' the life-giving book of the Gospels in the church. Het'um explains:

'It is necessary to explain the reason for writing this Gospel. At the time we have reached, all the world is suffering like a man who has aged and has reached the end of his life; he suffers because the strength of his limbs has diminished and he laments the loss of his senses. In the same way, because the world has aged, the action of good has decreased and the fire of evil has grown and spread, so the different parts of the universe suffer from chagrin.'

Het'um characterizes the Gospel's life-giving qualities thus:

'Because the Gospel is a herald of promises, of joyful enjoyments and the dignity of life without sorrow, it [the Gospel] announces the coming down of God to earth and the rising of man to heaven; it speaks to humankind about sharing life with the angels; it communicates the divine virtues that Jesus planted on earth. This is exactly what the place of the Gospel is in the divine liturgy.'

Given the great cost of producing manuscripts, the relative scarcity of books in contrast to the great demand for them, and the deep sense of veneration with which manuscripts were regarded, scribes beseeched the owners of manuscripts, whether individuals or ecclesiastical institutions, not to regard them as saleable merchandise or objects to be mortgaged. As a result, manuscripts frequently state that they are 'free and clear' from any monetary obligation, or that they were acquired by their commissioner or sponsor with *halal* (honestly earned) assets. For instance, the scribe of Matenadaran ms. No. 7446 writes:

'No one has the authority
To mortgage this for silver,
Or to sell it for money,
For it is few in all respects.'

Scribes also placed moral obligations on future generations to rescue manuscripts carried off as booty, by ransom or other means. In the Middle Ages, captured manuscripts were never referred to as booty, but rather, like human beings, they were either 'carried off into captivity' or were 'rescued or purchased from captivity'. The scribe of a Gospel manuscript copied by Kostandin in

1413 and given to the Church of the Holy Sepulchre in Jerusalem gives the following injunction to his readers:

'Let no one remove it from this place,
Let no one hand it over to an infidel.
Should there be any fear from the Muslims,
Let them put it in safe-keeping in the fort,
Or take it to the island of Cyprus;
And when the danger has passed,
Bring it back to this place,
And receive their fitting reward.'

In a Gospel dated 1411 (Mat. ms. No. 5510) the colophon states: 'I, T'agwor, and my sons Dscrun, Nikoghayos, Khatchatur and Dawit' have seen this book a prisoner of the Turks, and we agreed and bought it in our memory and in the memory of our parents.' At the end of the famous Queen Keran Gospels dated 1283, a note inserted in 1626 confirms people's awareness of the unique value of the manuscript: 'Remember again the unworthy Awk'send...I have consumed my life for thirty years in valleys and hills, I have lost wife and children, but I have managed to rescue this holy Gospel' (Mat. ms. No. 6764).

The various violations of injunctions concerning the proper treatment of manuscripts compelled many scribes or commissioners to record strict rules and to pronounce anathemas against violators. As early as the year 989, we read in the colophon of a Gospel: 'And let no one dare to remove for any reason this Word of God from this holy church at Noravank; and should anyone dare to remove this Gospel from the holy altar, may the usurper like Satan be denied the grace bestowed by the Son of God, and may his soul and flesh be cursed and may he, like the infidels who commit sacrilege, be condemned by the Son of God.' The scribe Avag, who copied a Gospel in 1337,

writes: 'should anyone dare to steal this holy Gospel, or tear off pages from it, or remove it from the great church of the holy and most immaculate monastery of Tat'ev, may he share the fate of Cain, Judas and the crucifiers and inherit the doleful maledections, amen.'

In order to perpetuate their memory, it was also customary for scribes or donors to request that their colophons be read in public on a specified day, as illustrated in the colophon of a Gospel written by its donor Awetik at Kaffa in the Crimea in 1456: 'Let this colophon be read every year on Palm Sunday; and may the individual, whether he be priest or layman, who acts contrary to this, be cursed by the power on high, and may he be denied participation in the divine liturgy in this church, and may he be accursed by all the saints, amen' (Mat. ms. No. 7831).

This tradition continues up to our own times. Among the manuscripts bequeathed to the British Library by the Hon. Robert Curzon through Baroness Darea Zouche on 13 October 1917 is a manuscript of the Bible copied in 1646. Among the uncanonical books, this Bible contains the History of Joseph and Asenath and III Paul to the Corinthians. In 1852 the then Lord Curzon invited the Armenian monk Ghewond Alishan (1820–1901) to Parham (Sussex), where he translated the *History of Joseph and Asenath* into Italian. This translation, together with the English rendered from the Italian by Robert Curzon himself, is now in the British Library (ms. BL Or. 15277), and has the following moving colophon by Ghewond Alishan:

'O thou who readest these lines of my handwriting, during the time of the present or of a future generation, remember me a passing pilgrim and think of thyself also, that thou art no less a pilgrim, whoever and whatever thou mayest be.'

Illuminations in Armenian Scriptures

'For what spoken narrative presents through hearing, this silent painting shows through imitation.'

St Basil of Caesarea (329–379)

'And what is the use of a book,' thought Alice, 'without pictures or conversations?'

Lewis Carroll, Alice's Adventures in Wonderland *(1865)*

Popular knowledge of the Bible is derived from its illustrations rather than its text. We all know, for example, that the ox and ass were present at the Nativity, but no one has acquired this information from the Gospels text, for it does not appear there: its source is the little-read apocryphal Gospel of pseudo-Matthew. We know about the ox and ass because they have appeared in illustrations of the Nativity since early Christian times, and continue to do so on modern Christmas cards. Equally, we know that Christ had long hair and a beard, not because he is so described in the Gospels, but because the Near-Eastern representation of Him proved more popular than the youthful, beardless type of early Christian Roman art, and became universally accepted throughout Christendom by the eleventh century.

Two basic facts emerge. First of all, there is our debt to the visual interpretation of the Bible as a factor often independent of and more powerful than the text itself. Secondly, pictures and text in manuscripts often travel together over long stretches of time, so the copying of one must obviously have a bearing on the other. St Nilus of Ancyra (d. 430), born in Constantinople and a student of the famous St John Chrysostom, approved the depiction of saints, but condemned the hunting scenes and the fauna as 'trifling and unworthy of a manly Christian soul' and suggested instead scenes from the Old and New Testaments 'painted by the hand of a gifted artist'. The Bible, he argued, set up on either side of the Holy Cross, would 'serve as books for the unlearned, teach

them scriptural history and impress on them the record of God's mercies'.

Complete Bibles do not provide the richest sources of biblical illustration. Extensive sets of pictures are found in copies of a single book or group of books, such as Genesis, or the Pentateuch. Books that contain drama and action would naturally provide more illustrative

22 ABOVE The Nativity and Adoration of the Magi, from the Gospels by Kararpet of Berkri, Van, late fifteenth century.
Trinity College, Dublin, ms. 10992, f.2r.

23 OPPOSITE The Letter of Eusebius to Carpianus explaining the Canon Tables, from the Gospels by Vardan Lehatsi, Aleppo, 1615.
The British Library, ms. Add.19549, ff.1v-2r.

material than the others. Unquestionably the most sumptous manuscripts of any part of the Bible illustrated up to the Middle Ages were the copies of the four Gospels bound in a single volume, frequently with splendid covers of ivory and silver gilt.

The contents of the Gospel books are fairly uniform. An important decorative feature is formed by the Canon Tables ascribed to Eusebius, Bishop of Caesarea (*c.* 260–*c.* 340). These tables were designed to show which passages in each of the individual gospels were in agreement with any of the other three. They are arranged in columns of figures under decorative arches, sometimes of great eleboration, and occasionally accompanied by scenes or symbols of the evangelists. They are to be found in all Christian traditions. Eusebius divides the Gospels into excerpts: Matthew 355, Mark 236, Luke 342, John 232. Within these divisions he divided the text into ten canons according to ten groupings, thus:

(1) Canon Matthew–Mark–Luke–John (71 parallels)
(2) Canon Matthew–Mark–Luke (111 parallels)
(3) Canon Matthew–Luke–John (22 parallels)
(4) Canon Matthew–Mark–John (26 parallels)
(5) Canon Matthew–Luke (80 parallels)
(6) Canon Matthew–Mark (8 parallels)
(7) Canon Matthew–John (7 parallels)
(8) Canon Luke–Mark (13 parallels)
(9) Canon Luke–John (21 parallels)
(10) Canon excerpts without parallels
    a. Matthew (61 without parallels)
    b. Mark (19 without parallels)
    c. Luke (73 without parallels)
    d. John (98 without parallels)

In most Armenian manuscripts each Gospel is prefaced by an introduction attributed to Ammonius, to whom Eusebius addresses his letter placed at the beginning of

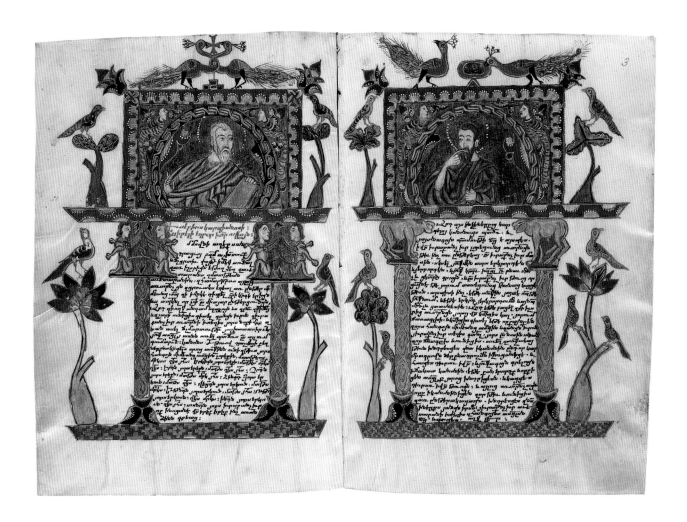

24 LEFT Portrait of St Matthew from the Gospels by Barsegh, Drazark monastery, Cilicia, 1282. *The British Library, ms. 5626, f.1v.*

25 BELOW Portrait and title-page of St Mark's Gospel from a manuscript painted by the artist Step'anos Vahkatsi (Sis, 1280) and restored by Mesrop Khizantsi (New Julfa, 1618). *The British Library, ms. Add.18549, ff.43v-44r.*

26 OPPOSITE The Portrait of St Luke and Theophilus holding a letter inscribed with the words 'and behold Jesus commandeth' from the Gospels copied for Marshal Oshin and illustrated by the artist Kostandin, Sis, Cilicia, thirteenth century. *Fitwilliam Museum, Cambridge, ms. McClean.201, f.3r.*

the Canon Tables. Before each Gospel is a miniature of the respective Evangelist, who is usually shown seated, though he may in some cases be standing. Incorporated into the portraits are the symbols of the evangelists. Matthew's symbol is an angel, Mark's a lion, Luke's an ox and John's an eagle. The symbols are explained so in the Gospel commissioned by Het'um I:

'The number four of the evangelists refers to the glorious throne of God [Ezekiel X: 14]...the human figure on the throne of God represents our rationality and is the symbol of the evangelist Matthew, who changed our word to the resemblance of the angels and accomplished the words of the evangelists. The figure of the lion represents the passion in us and

symbolizes the evangelist Mark, by whose teaching our passions were taken under control and directed against evil and toward good deeds. The ox inside us reflects the desires and, among the evangelists, Luke. It teaches us to use our right-mindedness in order to direct our desires toward the spiritual and the divine, and, in imitation of Christ and the fatted calf [Luke XV: 27], to sacrifice our earthly members. The form of the eagle on the throne of God represents the sense of justice in us and knowledge of the truth, by which we are elevated to heaven, and like the evangelist John, we thunder from the heights.'

The early practice in Greek manuscripts was to insert frameless illustrations whenever the text required them,

27 OPPOSITE Portraits of the four Evangelists from the Gospels by Melk'isedek, Berkri, north-eastern shore of Lake Van, 1338.
Matenadaran, Erevan, ms. 4813, f.5v.

28 RIGHT The Letter of Eusebius to Carpianus, instead of being written under architectural frames (see plate 23), is written in quatrefoil, framed by an ornate circular band. From the Avag Vank' Gospels by the scribe Vardan, Mount Sepuh, south of Erzindjan, 1200–02. The four-line note at the bottom in *notrgir* (cursive) hand was added in 1608: it concerns the command of Sultan Ahmed I (1603–17) to expel the Christians from the town of Erzindjan.
The British Library, ms. Or.13654, f.1v.

29 BELOW LEFT The title-page of St Mark's Gospel from the Gospels by T'oros Tarōnatsi, Gladzor monastery, Cilicia, 1321. In the middle of the head-piece the artist has depicted the Virgin enthroned and nursing the infant Jesus. The lion of St Mark forms the letter 'S' of the initial word of the Gospel '*Skizbn*' (Beginning), while the decoration in the outer margin is composed of the four symbols of the Evangelists.
The British Library, ms. Add.15411, f.92r.

30 BELOW RIGHT Ezekiel's Vision on the River Chebar shows four creatures carrying the chariot of God. In the lower right corner an angel feeds the prophet with a scroll. From the Erznka Bible of 1269.
St James's Monastery, Jerusalem, ms. 1925, f.414v.

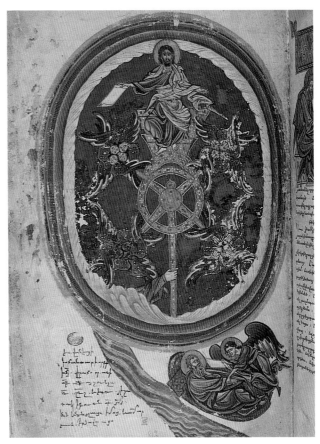

at the beginning of the pericope, or spiritual readings sometimes as many as 750 or 500 (for example Laurenziana Cod. Plut.VI.23 or BN Cod.gr.74). Patriarch Nicephoros (*c.* 758–829), when commenting on such prolifically illustrated manuscripts, refers to the 'spoken word' and the 'painted word', the painting giving a parallel account to that of the text. Perhaps so as not to distract the Gospel reader and to economize on space, at an early stage of development the pictures were taken out of the text and placed either in the margin or assembled at the beginning of the individual books.

The illumination of manuscripts in Armenia must have started soon after the invention of the Armenian alphabet, but the first stages of its history – from the fifth to the eighth centuries – remain unclear because no illuminated manuscripts have survived. In a treatise called *Yaghags Patkeramartits* (Concerning the Iconoclasts) the Armenian author Vrt'anes K'ert'ogh (550–620) refers to sumptuous gospels found in Armenia: 'We also see the book of the gospels painted and bound not only with gold and silver but with ivory and purple parchment.' K'ert'ogh is referring to the Greek manuscripts brought to Armenia from Constantinople for use by translators in the fifth and sixth centuries. From what we know of the major surviving purple codices – the Rossano and Sinope Gospels, and the Vienna Genesis – all date to the mid-sixth century. The ivory covers that bind the Ejmiadsin Gospels today, Byzantine works of the sixth century, are probably surviving relics from the time of Vrt'anes and provide eloquent testimony to the accuracy of his statements.

The earliest surviving Armenian illuminations, the final four miniatures of the Ejmiadsin Gospels – two leaves painted on each side, stitched on a pair of stubs at the end of the text before the colophon – originated from an older manuscript. On the basis of style, Professor S. Der Nersessian has convincingly attributed their provenance to the 'sphere of Armenian painting prior to the Arab invasion of 640'. The four valuable New Testament miniatures – the Annunciation to Zachariah, the Annunciation to the Virgin Mary, the Adoration of the Magi and Christ's Baptism (folios 228, 228b, 229, 229b) – all expound pictorially the theme of New Testament revelation. The unifying theme of the four miniatures in the Ejmiadsin Gospels is the feast of the

31 ABOVE Christ wipes the right foot of Peter, who is seated on a high stool and points to his head. From the Gospels by Avag, Sultaniya, 1329–58. *The British Library, ms. Or. 5304 f.65r.*

32 RIGHT Presentation of Christ in the Temple from the Gospels by the artist Step'anos, New Julfa, Isfahan, 1608. *The British Library, ms. 5737, f.4r.*

Epiphany, the celebration of which on 6 January opens the Armenian Church calendar, embracing the birth and baptism of Jesus as told in the Gospel readings selected for the occasion.

In a survey of illuminated Armenian manuscripts to the year 1000, the following tabular results are obtained:

The Sacrifice of Isaac (3 miniatures)
The Annunciation to the High Priest (1)
The Annunciation to the Virgin (2)

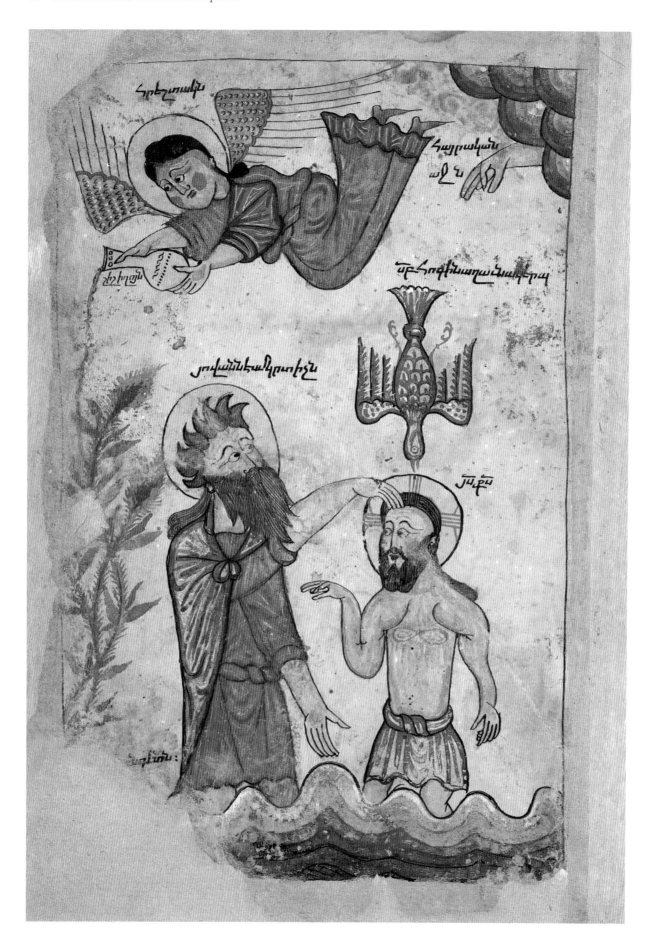

33 OPPOSITE The Baptism of Christ, from the Gospels by the artist Yovannes Khizantsi, Khizan, Gamaghiel, 1335.
Bibliothèque Nationale, Paris, ms. Arm. 333, f.3v.

34 LEFT The Raising of Lazarus, from the Gospels by the priest Karapet, Bzhnunik, Khlat, 1542.
The British Library, ms. Or.2707, f.14r.

35 BELOW Christ's Entry into Jerusalem, from the Gospels copied by the scribe Astuadsatur, Karbi, 1317.
The British Library, ms. Or.2680, f.4r.

The Nativity limited to the Adoration of the Magi (1)
Christ's Baptism (2)
The Crucifixion (1)
The Ascension (1)

Within the wide range of methods used in Gospel illumination in Byzantine and Eastern Christian art, the 'classic Armenian' method constitutes a unique contribution. As represented in the manuscripts of the eleventh century, the Armenian type consists of a set of full-page scenes which follow the Canon Tables and which are in turn followed by portraits of the Evangelists, the four often grouped together on a single page. This scheme of illustration continued to be used in Armenian manuscripts down the centuries, even though other models were known and used.

According to Tiatiana A. Izmailova, the most extensive cycle of pictures representing the life of Jesus Christ are found in a group of manuscripts belonging to the school of Melitene dated 1041 and 1057 (Jerusalem ms. No. 3624 and Matenadaran ms. No. 3784). The twelve miniatures are:

The Annunciation
The Nativity
The Presentation in the Temple
The Baptism of Jesus
The Transfiguration
The Raising of Lazarus
The Entry into Jerusalem
The Last Supper
The Betrayal of Judas
The Crucifixion
The Descent into Hell
The Ascension

The iconographical programme no doubt comprised a series of miniatures depicting the major dominical feasts.

36 ABOVE The Washing of the Feet, the Last Supper, the Betrayal by Judas, Peter cutting the servant's ear and denying Christ to the servant girl. From the Gospels by Rstakes, Khizan, 1397.
Matenadaran, Erevan, ms. 7629, f.267.

37 RIGHT Descent into Hell, from the lectionary by Zak'aria, Crimea, 1631.
The British Library, ms. Or.15291, f.211v.

38 OPPOSITE The Entombment of Christ, from the Gospels by the priest Avetik', monastery of St George, Balu, 1437.
The British Library, ms. Or.2668, f.5v.

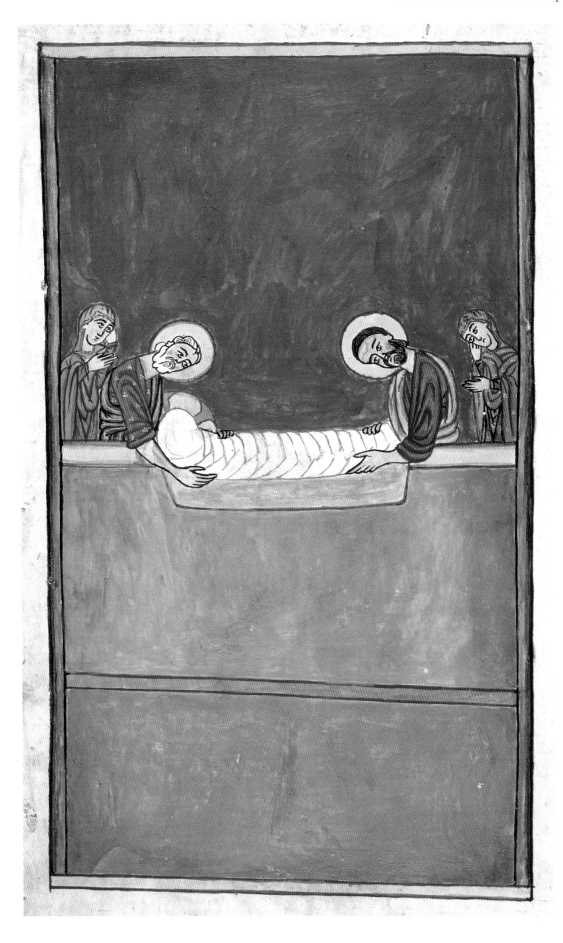

39 ABOVE The Holy Women at the Empty Tomb
with the Risen Christ, from the Gospels by the
artist Ewagris, Taron, 1038.
Matenadaran, Erevan, ms. 6201, f.8r.

40 OPPOSITE The Descent of the Holy Spirit at
Pentecost, from the Gospels painted by the artist
Nikoghayos, Crimea, 1658.
The British Library, ms. Or. 13895, f.13a.

ՎԱՍՆ ՀՈԳՈՅՆ ԳԱԼՈՒՍՏՆ.

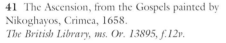

41 The Ascension, from the Gospels painted by
Nikoghayos, Crimea, 1658.
The British Library, ms. Or. 13895, f.12v.

42 The Last Judgement, with Christ on a throne
supported by the symbols of the Evangelists, with
the Virgin and St John the Baptist at the sides, and
the figures of the patrons Ter Yohannes and Ter
Step'anos. From the Gospels by Karapet of
Berkri, Lake Van, late fifteenth century.
Trinity College Dublin, ms. 10992, f.11r.

In the Middle Byzantine period a set of twelve pictures
had been selected in church decorations as well as in icon
painting, but it must be stated that there is nothing
canonical about the number twelve and the cycle is
extended to include additional topics. For instance, the
pictures of Holy Week are extended to include the
Washing of the Feet, the Hearing before Pilate, the
Deposition from the Cross, the Resurrection, Pentecost,
the Harrowing of Hell, the Glorification of the Cross,
and the Last Judgement.

The Nature of Image Veneration in Armenia

Armenian painting, being essentially Christian, had to represent what is intangible and imperceptible and to narrate in colour and line the events drawn from the earthly life of Jesus. The paintings were never gratuitous but always functional, since the religious images were created to enable the believer to apprehend the divine and follow visually the life story of Jesus. The efficiency of the image did not depend upon realism but upon the representation of what was recognized as the principle of the things portrayed and as the thinking of the Armenian Church.

Exegesis, the work of explaining the sacred scriptures, was one of the chief occupations in the monastic schools of Armenia. A vivid picture of a monastic classroom is provided by a miniature in a commentary on Isaiah copied in 1301, now in the library of St James's, Jerusalem (see plate 18). The image shows Esayi Ntchetsi, abbot of the monastery at Gladzor, instructing a group of monks. A stream of heavenly inspiration flows into his ear and out of his mouth to his pupils, many of whom hold their own copy of the sacred scriptures wrapped in a handkerchief. The copy on which Esayi comments is read by a monk kneeling in the centre.

A set of Gospel miniatures should be regarded as a visual commentary on the text. This is not to belittle the inventiveness of individual artists or to underestimate the importance of stylistic change. Different ages found inspiration in different parts of the Bible, and doctrinal changes and biblical commentaries affected the appearance of the illustrations.

In an Armenian menologium, or calendar of the saints (see plate 43), the Annunciation is depicted twice in one miniature: in one scene the Virgin Mary is shown at the well with a jar of water, while the other shows her in the house with the spirit descending. The miniature illustrates not the Gospel story but the apocryphal Protevangelium in which Mary and other virgins are given the task of weaving a veil for the temple. The purple and the scarlet parts of the veil are alloted to Mary. She hears a voice at the well calling her highly favoured and blessed among women. She looks to her left and right and sees no one. Trembling, she returns home and puts down her pitcher. She takes up the purple thread to go on with her weaving and suddenly sees the angel near her. She hears him say: 'Don't be afraid, for you have found favour with the Lord of all things, and you shall conceive his Word.'

A miniature of the Death of the Virgin, painted by T'oros Taronatsi in the four Gospels dated 1311 (see plate 44), represents a tale told of Mary in a sermon of the monk Epiphanius, that 'after a little, while all who were present watched, the body become invisible before our eyes'. A house is attacked and burnt, but Mary is rescued by Christ, the apostles and angels, and carried through the air to her Dormition on Zion, where more apostles come on clouds to join them, some from their graves, for a deathbed scene, where Christ receives her soul. A funeral procession follows to the valley of the Kedron and the garden of Gethsemane.

Finally, a miniature of the Magi in the same menologium (see plate 43) is based not on the Gospels but the *Armenian Infancy Gospels*. The three Magi who visit the Christ Child, each had a different vision of him, which they realized only later when comparing stories about him. Gaspar reported seeing a child, 'Son of God incarnate, seated on a throne of glory'. Balthasar saw him as commander of the heavenly forces 'seated on an exalted throne before whom a countless army fell down and adored'. Finally, Melk'on saw him dying in torment, rising and returning to life. Trying twice to resolve the differences, they each had the visions of the other two. These three views have led to the iconographic tradition of depicting the three Magi as men of different ages – young, middle-aged and old.

For centuries, many Christian communions and historians have accused the Armenian Church of being iconoclastic. Very often during the historical growth and

43 LEFT At the top, the
Annunciation is depicted twice.
On the far left the Virgin is
shown outside holding a water
pitcher. On the near left she is
shown indoors wearing the veil
and receiving the news from the
angel. In the Adoration of the
Magi three men represent three
different ages, young, middle-
aged and old. From *The Lives
of the Saints*, Constantinople,
1652.
*The British Library, ms.
Or.12550, f.257v.*

44 RIGHT The Dormition
of the Virgin Mary from the
Gospels painted by T'oros
Taronatsi. The artist added his
own portrait lower right. He is
shown wearing deacon's robes
and holding a censer and small
incense box, apparently taking
part in the burial of the Virgin.
His name is inscribed near
his head. From the Four
Gospels, 1311.
*The Chester Beatty Library,
Dublin, ms. Arm.559, f.1r.*

development of the Church in Armenia, religious movements, such as the Paulicians and the T'ondrakians, emerged and taught an iconoclastic doctrine, which was not the theology and doctrine of the Church. But from the earliest days, images and icons always had an important place in expressing the devotion and piety of the faithful.

The Church adopted devotional piety from pagan worship, and sanctified it in Christianity by the sacrament of *The order of consecration of painted pictures in the church*. Several Armenian Church fathers, including Vrt'anes K'ert'ogh, Step'anos Siwnetsi, Yovhan Odznetsi, Nerses Shnorhali, Grigor Tat'evatsi, Matt'eos *vardapet* Jughayetsi and Ghukas Vanandetsi, have often reflected in their theological writings on the role of art in worship, and defended its veneration. The first and most lucid justification of icons and images and explanation of their purpose in the Armenian Church and theology was written by Vrt'anes K'eret'ogh:

'When we bow before the Holy Gospel, or when we kiss it, we do not worship the ivory or the red paint... but we worship the word of the Saviour written on the parchment.'

'...It is not because of the colours that we prostrate ourselves before the images but because of Christ in whose name they are painted.'

'...we attain the invisible through what is visible, and the pigments and pictures are memorials of the living God and his Servants.'

Nerses Shnorhali teaches that in spite of the fallen state of man he is still in 'the image of God, and paradise is his habitation'. He proposes that the whole world of experience may be divided into two classes of objects: the necessary and the pleasurable or sensuous. Such a distinction was commonplace among Christian authors struggling with the problem of religious art, who used the distinction to denigrate the pleasurable or the sensuous. Hypatius of Ephesus, for example, says, 'for our part, we take no pleasure whatever in any sculpture or painting. However, we permit simple folk, inasmuch as they are less perfect, to learn such things in an introductory manner by means of sight, which is appropriate to their natural development, having found on many occasions that even the old and new ordinances of God may be brought down to the level of the weaker for the sake of their spiritual salvation.'

St Nilus of Ancyra described certain ideal features of ecclesiastical decoration in one of his many letters. While approving the depiction of saints, he condemned the hunting scenes and the fauna as 'trifling and unworthy of a manly Christian soul' and suggested instead scenes from Old and New Testaments 'painted by the hand of a gifted artist'. These, he argued, set up on either side of the Holy Cross, would 'serve as books for the unlearned, teach them spiritual history and impress on them the record of God's mercies'.

Two centuries later, Pope Gregory the Great (*c.* 540–604) would echo the views of St Nilus: 'It is one thing to worship a picture, it is another to learn in depth, by means of pictures, a venerable story. For that which writing makes clear to the reader, pictures make known to the illiterate because in pictures the ignorant see the story they ought to follow, and those who don't know their letters find that they can, after a fashion, read. Therefore, especially for the common folk, pictures are the equivalent of reading.'

For Nerses Shnorhali, however, the situation is exactly the reverse. In his commentary on the ten Canon Tables he gives the following interpretation to each canon:

1. God Almighty
2/3. Middle and last priesthood of the angels
4. Paradise
5. Noah's Ark
6. Altar of Abraham
7/8. Holy of Holies of Moses
9. Temple of Solomon
10. The Holy Church 'which encompasses the mysteries of all'.

The sensual pleasures of the Canon Tables are not designed for simple or uneducated folk but rather for 'perfected' ones, namely the initiated. Pleasures, he says, 'which are not accounted important, are of great utility to perfected ones, when by this manifest colour, taste,

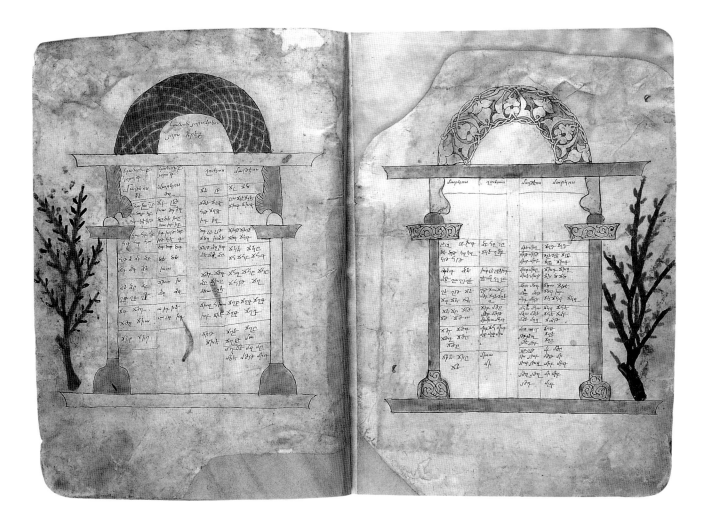

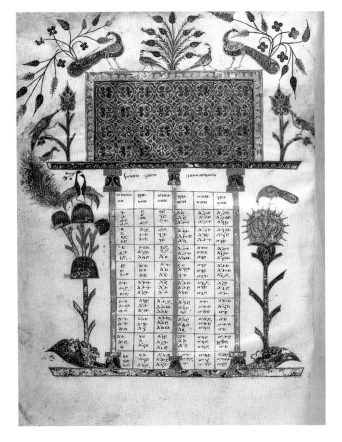

45 ABOVE Canon Tables from the Gospels by Astuadsatur, Karbi, Vaspurakan, 1317. *The British Library, ms. Or.2680, f.7v-8r.*

46 LEFT Canon Tables from the Avag Vank' Gospels by Vardan *dpir*, Mount Sepuh, south-west of Erzindjan, 1200–02. *The British Library, ms. Or.13654, f.5r.*

47 OVERLEAF Canon Tables Nos. vii–viii, from the Gospels by Mesrop Khizantsi, Isfahan, 1608. The two horns represent Moses and Aaron. *The British Library, ms. Or.5737, ff.24v-25r.*

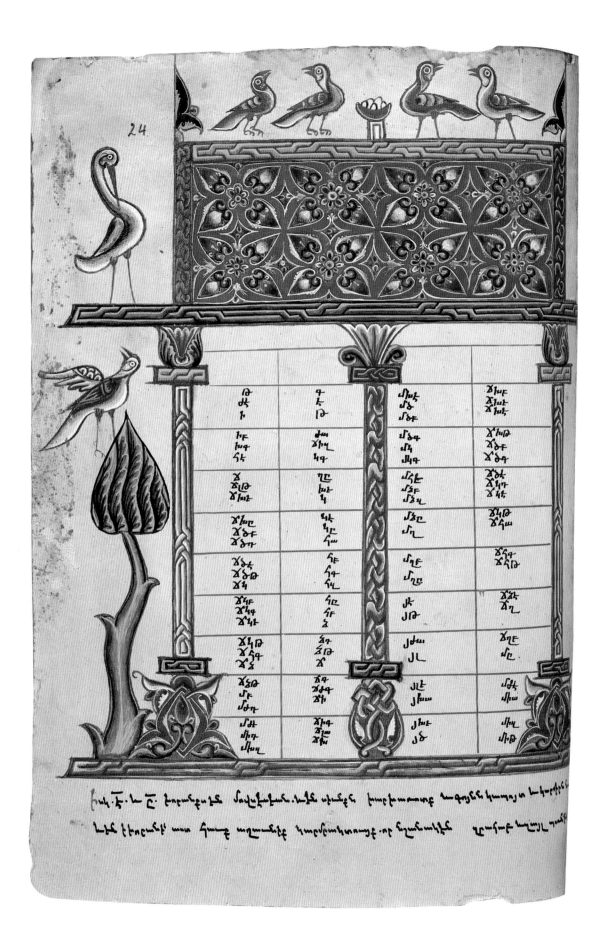

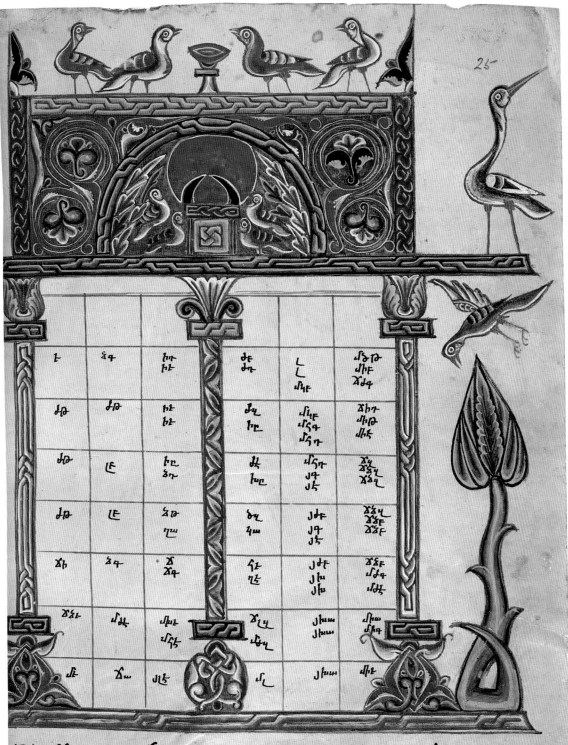

smell, hearing and the rest we ascend to the spiritual and to the rational enjoyment of the good tidings of God, which eye has not seen and ear has not heard, and which the heart of man has not recalled, which God has prepared for his loved ones.' Nerses calls the Canon Tables 'baths of sight and hearing for those approaching the soaring peaks of God'. In brief, the ornamented pages become an instrument of meditation, preparing the soul by focusing the viewer's attention on largely abstract forms and colours. The Canon Tables were meant to focus the powers of the soul on the central mysteries of Christian revelation. Two premises lie behind such an approach. The first premise is the frank acceptance of the sensuous as something good in itself and therefore worthy of serious attention from the intellectual. According to Nerses, 'God gave the lover of material things understanding of the heavenly.' The second premise is that the most profound meanings contained in the Canon Tables must be left hidden. This is the exact opposite of the symbolic systems of Western medieval art, which is didactic in intent and depends on spelling out all meanings explicitly, thus removing all mystery. For Nerses the Canon Tables must convey the 'mystical' and the 'mysterious', for in the end 'the mystery is apparent only to a few, and in its entirety only to God'.

Emphasized in the several unique sources of medieval art theory and criticism published by V. Ghazarian, but poorly represented in the written records of Byzantine art, is the doctrine of colour. Red, green, black and blue, which signify the four elements of light, earth, water and air, are most important. To these four colours Grigor Tat'ewatsi adds 'gold', the fifth 'substance of heaven... the symbol of divine light'. These 'all magnificent' colours aim at approaching the 'promised spiritual delights', as Paul the Apostle puts it, not seen by the eye, not heard by the ear, nor felt by a human heart. The concept of iconology is 'well proportioned altars, decorated temples, and gold, and pearls, and magnificent gems'. This is summed up in the following prayer recited by the priest at the beginning of Mass:

'In the midst of this temple, and before these god-receiving and thus made resplendent holy signs [i.e. Gospel and Cross], we bow down in fear and worship.'

The Bible in Armenian Piety and Worship

Alexander Pushkin, according to Vladimir Nabokov in the foreword to his translation of *Eugene Onegin*, 'likened translations to horses changed at the posthouse of civilization'. Translation has been a crucial process in world culture over the last two or three millennia, and perhaps especially so in Armenian culture, which was shaped by the translation of the Bible. In order to make this point, in 1935, on the 1500th anniversary of the translation of the Bible into Armenian, Professor N.Adontz compared the role of the Armenian Bible with that of the Vulgate in Latin literature. 'The Latin Vulgate,' he writes, 'did not have the same importance to the Latin countries as the Armenian Bible to the Armenian people. Latin literature had been in existence for a long time when the Vulgate appeared, whereas the Armenian Bible heralded a new era in which the Armenian people learning for the first time the use of the pen came to take their place in the civilized world.' F.C. Conybeare, the noted English biblical scholar, was deeply convinced of the high value of the Armenian translation: 'for beauty of diction and accuracy of rendering, the Armenian cannot be surpassed. The genius of the language is such as to render the translation of any Greek document both literal and graceful – true to the order of the Greek, and even reflecting its compound words, yet without being slavish, and without violence to its own idiom. We are seldom in doubt as to what stood in the Armenian's Greek text; therefore the Armenian version has almost the same value for us as the Greek text itself, from which he worked, would possess. The same is true of the Armenian New Testament as well.' Much earlier the French scholar M. de la Croze (1661–1719) called it 'the Queen of the Versions'. Georges Cuendet, a former professor of the University of Geneva, also remarked on its accuracy: 'The Armenian version, remarkable from every point of view, is an original masterpiece. One does not know where to fault these writers, so exceptional was their penetration, so great their mastery of the subject. They undertook to nationalize the translation of the Bible, and they succeeded to such a degree that the whole of the Armenian literature goes back to this source.'

Soon after the translation of the Bible into Armenian, the historian P'awstos Buzand reported that 'the ranks of the scribes were increased' and 'old and young, succoured and filled with spiritual profit, ran joyfully from participation in the great mystery [Divine Liturgy] back to their houses, singing psalms and antiphons everywhere, in the squares and streets and at home'. In Armenian learning and literature, the bible takes pride of place and knowledge of the scriptures was the prime qualification. Armenian authors used biblical imagery, quotations, made allusions to biblical authors and embellished their narratives with biblical material as a matter of course. Eghishē, author of *The History of Vardan and the Armenian War Fought in 451*, testifies that Vardan the commander was himself 'learned in holy scriptures from his youth'. P'awstos Buzand presents Vardan as 'a learned man versed in scripture – for he was very erudite and familiar with the teaching of scripture, having been instructed and educated by the holy patriarch Sahak, his grandfather'. In an exhortation to the army on the eve of the battle in 451, Vardan gave a resumé of the story of the Maccabees: 'Taking up the brave model of the Maccabees, he read it out to them all, telling them in fluent words of the outcome of events – how they had fought and struggled against the king of Antioch for their God-given religion.'

In preparation for the war, Eghishē reported that 'the

voices of the ministers ceased not day and night from reciting the holy Psalms. The readers of the divine scriptures never paused at any hour, neither did the expounders of the consolation of heavenly teaching.' For the women who had stayed home, 'Psalms were perpetually murmured on their lips, and readings from the prophets were their supreme consolation.' Throughout the night before the battle the army prayed and, in the words of P'awstos Buzand, 'groups of priests, with the psalms and words of instruction, encouraged the soldiers to be valiant and inherit unfailing blessings'. Every man and priest was a church in himself. Their bodies were holy altars and their souls worthy offerings: 'Psalms were their whispering songs and the reading of the holy scriptures their absolute joy.' The Vardanians were ready for torture and death 'since we recognize the holy Gospel to be our father and the Apostolic Church our mother; let no evil meddler try to separate us from her'. This, Eghishē concludes, is because all Christians together are united by virtue of a sacred word and their Covenant with the Lord'.

The Armenian word *ukht* (covenant), used to render the Hebrew word *berith* and the Greek *diatheke*, is also used in the titles of the two parts of the Bible – Hin Ukht and Nor Ukht, meaning the Old Covenant and the New Covenant, which better convey an understanding of what the Bible contains. Loyalty of the soldiers to God's covenant was 'sworn and sealed with a fearsome oath on the holy gospel' and those who abandoned the union were 'false to God's covenant and had deceitfully violated the oath'. The historian Step'anos Taronatsi reports that a monk named Sargis from the monastery of Hndzut in Karin 'sang the psalms of David night and day', while another monk from Aghwank' was reputed to know the whole Bible by heart. Another historian, T'ovmay Ardsruni (840–960), mentions the Armenian general Gurgen Ardsruni, who before going into battle with the Arabs 'raised his hands to heaven with tears and prayed, reciting Psalms 34 and 82'.

The Four Gospels is the chief liturgical book of the Armenian Church, a fact reflected in the splendour of its miniatures and delicate repoussé covers. It is always placed on the altar next to the holy cross. During the divine liturgy the deacon receives the book from the priest, raises it up and says, 'Proskhoumē' [Be attentive].

48 OPPOSITE Penitent David, with his harp at his feet and his Psalter and crown on a canopy before him, kneels in prayer in his chamber, while God looks down from the top right-hand corner. From the Bible by Malnazar and Aghap'ir, New Julfa, Isfahan, 1637–8.
J. Paul Getty Museum, ms. Ludwig I 14, f.320v.

49 RIGHT Christ enthroned and surrounded by the symbols of the four Evangelists. He blesses and holds the Gospels in his left hand. From the Gospels by Partagh, Cilicia, 1239.
British and Foreign Bible Society, Cambridge, ms. 77, f.7v.

50 The Gospels copied by Partagh in 1239, was renewed and bound by Step'anos as memorial to himself in 1427. The top cover has four medallions representing four events from the Gospels: Resurrection, Crucifixion, Baptism and Annunciation. Chased into the corners of the metal panel are four more medallions, each bearing one of the symbols of the Evangelists. The lower cover represents Mary, Mother of God with the Child who is holding a globe in his hand. It is possible that the binding is of East European origin. *British and Foreign Bible Society, Cambridge, ms. 77.*

The deacon then processes round the altar followed by fan-bearers, returns to the front, then lowers the book to let the senior clegyman kiss it. While the procession takes place, the choir sings the Trisagion ['thrice Holy'] and the priest silently says the following prayer:

> 'O Lord our God, who hast established in the heavens the orders and the hosts of angels and archangels for the ministry of thy glory, make now the holy angels also enter with our entrance and serve with us and glorify with us thy goodness.'

Belief in the 'real presence' of Christ throughout the service is symbolized by the Gospel. Before reading the lesson from the Gospels, selections are read from the Old Testament and the Epistles from the chancel in the nave. The Gospel is always read by the priest celebrating the Mass or by a deacon, who instructs the congregation to stand and begins the reading by declaring, 'God speaks'. The sermon preached after the reading of the Gospel was originally meant to be a commentary on what had been read in the lessons. After this the whole congregation confirms its faith by reciting the Nicene Creed.

The Gospel is the only book venerated in the Armenian Church, and every ritual is blessed by the priest, who holds the book and chants, 'Blessed and protected...by the sign of the holy cross and by the holy Gospel'.

In a manuscript of the Gospels written in 1064 (Jerusalem, No. 1924), Martiros Baberdatsi, who had the manuscript restored in memory of his parents, added a versed doxology, the first verse of which translates:

> 'I praise you Holy Gospel
> You are dwelling of God,
> For us sinners fortress of hope
> Place of expiation for penitents.'

Appendix 1: The Canon of the Bible

Books of the Old Testament in Hebrew	Books of the Old Testament in Septuagint Greek	Books of the Old Testament in Vulgate Latin	Books of the New Testament
Genesis	Genesis	Genesis	St Matthew
Exodus	Exodus	Exodus	St Mark
Numbers	Leviticus	Leviticus	St Luke
Deuteronomy	Numbers	Numbers	St John
Joshua	Deuteronomy	Deuteronomy	Acts of the Apostles
Judges	Joshua	Joshua	Epistle to the Roman
I Samuel	Judges	Judges	I Epistle to the Corinthians
II Samuel	Ruth	I Kings (= I Samuel)	II Epistle to the Corinthians
I Kings	I Kingdoms	II Kings (= II Samuel)	Epistle to the Galatians
II Kings	II Kingdoms	III Kings (= I Kings)	Epistle to the Ephesians
Isaiah	III Kingdoms	IV Kings (= II Kings)	Epistle to the Phillippians
Jeremiah	IV Kingdoms	I Paralipomena (= I	Epistle to the Colossians
Ezekiel	I Paralipomena	Chronicles)	I Epistle to the Thessalonians
Hosea	(= I Chronicles)	II Paralipomena (= II Chronicles)	II Epistle to the Thessalonians
Joel	II Paralipomena	I Esdras (= Hebews + Ezra)	I Epistle to Timothy
Amos	(= II Chronicles)	II Esdras (= Hebrews + Nehemiah	II Epistle to Timothy
Obadiah	I Esdras	III Esdras (= Greek I Esdras)	Epistle to Titus
Jonah	II Esdras (= Ezra + Nehemiah)	IV Esdras	Epistle to Philemon
Micah	Esther	Tobit	Epistle to the Hebrews
Nahum	Tobit	Judith	Epistle of St James
Habakkuk	I Maccabees	Esther	I Epistle of St Peter
Zephaniah	II Maccabees	Job	II Epistle of St Peter
Haggai	III Maccabees	Psalms	I Epistle of St John
Zechariah	IV Maccabees	Proverbs	II Epistle of St John
Malachi	Psalms	Ecclesiastes	III Epistle of St John
Psalms	Odes of Solomon	Song of Songs	Epistle of St Jude
Job	Proverbs of Solomon	Wisdom	Book of the Apocalypse (Revelations)
Proverbs	Ecclesiastes	Ecclesiasticus	
Ruth*	Song of Songs		

Books of the Old Testament in Hebrew	Books of the Old Testament in Septuagint Greek	Books of the Old Testament in Vulgate Latin	Books of the New Testament
Song of Songs*	Job	Isaiah	
Ecclesiastes*	Wisdom of Solomon	Jeremiah	
Lamentations*	Ecclesiasticus	Lamentations	
Esther*	Psalms of Solomon	Baruch	
Daniel	Hosea	Ezekiel	
Ezra**	Amos	Daniel	
I Chronicles	Micah	Hosea	
II Chronicles	Joel	Joel	
	Obadiah	Amos	
*The 'Five Rolls' read on certain festivals	Jonah	Obadiah	
	Nahum	Jonah	
	Habakkuk	Micah	
**Later divided Ezra,	Zephaniah	Nahum	
Nehemiah	Haggai	Habakkuk	
	Zechariah	Zephaniah	
	Malachi	Haggai	
	Isaiah	Zechariah	
	Jeremiah	Malachi	
	Baruch (= I:5)	I Maccabees	
	Lamentations	II Maccabees (Prayer of Manasses)	
	Letter of Jeremiah (= Baruch VI)		
	Ezekiel		
	Daniel (= Susanna + Hebrews		
	Daniel + 'Bel and the Dragon')		
	Prayer of Manasses		

Appendix 2: The Canon of the Armenian Bible

Anania Shirakatsi Seventh century	**Sarkavag** *vardapet* **Mkhitar Ayrevanetsi** Twelfth to thirteenth centuries	**Grigor Tat`evatsi** Fourteenth century
Genesis	Genesis	Genesis
Exodus	Exodus	Exodus
Leviticus	Leviticus	Leviticus
Numbers	Numbers	Numbers
Deuteronomy	Deuteronomy	Deuteronomy
Joshua Nehemiah	Joshua Nehemiah	Joshua
Judges	Judges	Judges
Ruth	Ruth	Ruth
I Kingdoms	I Kingdoms	I Kingdoms
II Kingdoms	II Kingdoms	II Kingdoms
III Kingdoms	III Kingdoms	III Kingdoms
IV Kingdoms	IV Kingdoms	IV Kingdoms
I Chronicles	I Chronicles	I Chronicles
II Chronicles	II Chronicles	II Chronicles
I Maccabees	I Ezra	I Ezra
II Maccabees	II Ezra	II Ezra
III Maccabees	I Maccabees	III Ezra
IV Maccabees	II Maccabees	Nehemiah
Hosea	III Maccabees	Esther
Amos	Enoch	Judith
Micah	Testaments	Tobit
Joel	Prayer of Asenath	I Maccabees
Obadiah	Tobit	II Maccabees
Jonah	Judith	III Maccabees
Nahum	Esther	Psalms
Habakkuk	III Ezra	Proverbs
Zephaniah	Job	Song of Songs
Haggai	Pslams	Ecclesiasticus
Zechariah	Hosea	Wisdom
Malachi	Amos	Sirach
Isaiah	Micah	Job
Jeremiah	Joel	Isaiah
Baruch	Obadiah	Hosea
Lamentations	Jonah	Amos
Letter of Jeremiah	Nahum	Micah
Ezekiel	Habakkuk	Joel
Daniel	Zephaniah	Obadiah
Psalms	Haggai	Jonah
Proverbs	Zechariah	Nahum
Ecclesiastes	Malachi	Habakkuk
Song of Songs	Proverbs	Zephania
Wisdom	Isaiah	Haggai
Job	Jeremiah	Zechariah
Sirach	Ezekiel	Malachi
I Erzra	Job	Jeremiah
II Ezra	Daniel	Baruch
Nehemia	III Chronicles	Lamentations

Anania Shirakatsi Seventh century	**Sarkavag** *vardapet* **Mkhitar Ayrevanetsi** Twelfth and thirteenth centuries	**Grigor Tat`evatsi** Fourteenth century
Esther	Letter of Jeremiah	Daniel
Tobit	XXIV Death of the Prophets	Ezekiel
Judith	Sirach	Testaments
Mathew	John	
Mark	Matthew	
Luke	Mark	Matthew
John	Luke	Mark
		Luke
Acts of the Apostles	Acts of the Apostles	John
James		
I Peter	James	Acts of the Apostles
II Peter	I Peter	James
I John	II Peter	I Peter
II John	I John	II Peter
III John	II John	I John
Jude	III John	II John
	Jude	III John
Revelations	Plea of Euthalius	Jude
Romans	Romans	Romans
I Corinthians	I Corinthians	I Corinthians
II Corinthians	II Corinthians	II Corinthians
Galatians	Letter of the Corinthians	Galatians
Ephesians	III Corinthians	Ephesians
Philippians	Galatians	Philippians
Colossians	Ephesians	Colossians
I Thessalonians	Philippians	I Thessalonians
II Thessalonians	Colossians	II Thessalonians
Hebrews	I Thessalonians	Hebrews
I Timothy	II Thessalonians	I Timothy
II Timothy	Hebrews	II Timothy
Titus	I Timothy	Titus
Philemon	II Timothy	Philemon
	Titus	III Corinthians
	Philemon	
		Taddeus
	Revelations	Reading from James
	Repose of St John	2nd Apostolic Canons
		Words of Justus
		Dionysius Aeropagite
		Preaching of St Peter

Appendix 3: Recensions of the Armenian Bible

Erznka, 1269	Cilicia, 1319	Baberdatsi, Lvov, 1619
	Preface to Genesis	Preface to Genesis
	Chapter of Genesis	Chapters of Genesis
Genesis	Genesis	Genesis
	Preface to Exodus	Preface to Exodus
	Chapter of Exodus	Chapters of Exodus
Exodus	Exodus	Exodus
	Preface to Leviticus	Preface to Leviticus
	Chapter of Leviticus	Chapters of Leviticus
Leviticus	Leviticus	Leviticus
	Preface to Numbers	Preface to Numbers
	Chapter of Numbers	Chapters of Numbers
Numbers	Numbers	Numbers
	Preface to Deuteronomy	Preface to Deuteronomy
	Chapters of Deuteronomy	Chapters of Deuteronomy
Deuteronomy	Deuteronomy	Deuteronomy
Joshua son of Nehemiah	Preface to Joshua	Preface to Joshua
	Chapter of Joshua	Chapters of Joshua
	Joshua	Joshua
	Preface to Judges	Preface to Judges
	Chapters of Judges	Chapters of Judges
		These are the Judges
Judges	Judges	Judges
	Preface to Ruth	Preface to Ruth
Ruth	Ruth	Ruth
	General preface to Kingdoms	General preface to Kingdoms
	Preface to Kingdoms	Preface to Kingdoms
	Chapters of I Kingdoms	Chapters of Kingdoms
I Kingdoms	I Kingdoms	I Kingdoms
	Chapters of II Kingdoms	Chapters of II Kingdoms
II Kingdoms	II Kingdoms	II Kingdoms
	Chapters of III Kingdoms	Chapters of III Kingdoms
III Kingdoms	III Kingdoms	III Kingdoms
	Chapters of IV Kingdoms	Chapters of IV Kingdoms
IV Kingdoms	IV Kingdoms	IV Kingdoms
	Preface to Chronicles I–II	Preface to I–II Chronicles
	Chapters of Chronicles I	Chapters of I Chronicles
I Chronicles	I Chronicles	I Chronicles
	Chapters of II Chronicles	Chapters of II Chronicles
II Chronicles	II Chronicles	II Chronicles
	Preface to I Ezra	Preface to I Ezra
	Chapters of I Ezra	Chapters of I Ezra
I Ezras	I Ezra	I Ezra
	Chapters of II Ezra	Chapters of II Ezra
II Ezras	II Ezra	II Ezra
		III Ezra
	Preface to Nehemiah	Preface to Nehemiah
	Chapters of Nehemiah	Chapters of Nehemiah
Nehemiah	Nehemiah	Nehemiah
Job	Preface to Esther	

Erznka, 1269	Cilicia, 1319	Baberdatsi, Lvov, 1619
		Preface to Esther
	Esther	
	Preface to Judith	Esther
	Judith	Preface to Judith
	Preface to Tobit	Judith
	Tobit	Preface to Tobit
	Preface to I Maccabees	Tobit
	Chapters of I Maccabees	Preface to I Maccabees
	I Maccabees	Chapters of I Maccabees
	Preface to II Maccabees	I Maccabees
	Chapters of II Maccabees	Preface to II Maccabees
	II Maccabees	Chapters of II Maccabees
	Preaface of III Maccabees	II Maccabees
	Chapters of III Maccabees	Preface to III Maccabees
	III Maccabees	Chapters of III Maccabees
Testament of Reuben		III Maccabees
Testament of Shmavon		Testament of Reuben
Testament of Levi		Testament of Shmavon
Testament of Judah		Testament of Levi
Testament of Issachar		Testament of Judah
Testament of Zebulun		Testament of Issachar
Testament of Dan		Testament of Zebulun
Testament of Naphtali		Testament of Dan
Testament of Gad		Testament of Naphtali
Testament of Asher		Testament of Gad
Testament of Joseph		Testament of Asher
Testament of Benjamin		Testament of Joseph
St Ephraem on Joseph		Testament of Benjamin
		Preface to Job
		Julian's preface
	Epiphanius's preface to Psalms	Job
	David Invbl's preface to Psalms	Epiphanius's preface to Psalms
	Psalms	
	Preface of Proverbs	Psalter
	Chapters of Proverbs	Preface to Proverbs
	Proverbs	Chapters of Proverbs
	Preface to Ecclesiasticus	Proverbs
	Chapters of Ecclesiasticus	Preface to Ecclesiasticus
	Ecclesiasticus	Chapters of Ecclesiasticus
	Preface to Song of Songs	Ecclesiasticus
	Song of Songs	
	Preface to Wisdom	Song of Songs
	Chapters of Wisdom	Preface to Wisdom
	Wisdom	Chapters of Wisdom
	Colophon of Nerses IV	Wisdom of Solomon
	Preface to Job	Wisdom of Sirach
	Preface to Julian	
	Job	
Chapters of Isaiah	Preface to Isaiah	
Isaiah	Chapters of Isaiah	Preface to Isaiah
	Isaiah	Chapters of Isaiah
	Death of Isaiah	Isaiah
Jeremiah		
Baruch		

Erznka, 1269	Cilicia, 1319	Baberdatsi, Lvov, 1619
Lamentations		
	Preface of the Twelve Prophets	Preface of the Twelve Prophets
	Chapters of Hosea	Chapters of Hosea
Hosea	Hosea	Hosea
Death of Hosea		Death of Hosea
	Chapters of Amos	Chapters of Amos
Amos	Amos	Amos
Death of Amos		Death of Amos
Micah	Chapters of Micah	Chapters of Micah
Death of Micah	Micah	Micah
		Death of Micah
Joel	Chapters of Joel	Chapters of Joel
Death of Joel	Joel	Joel
		Death of Joel
Obadiah	Chapters of Obadiah	Chapters of Obadiah
Death of Obadiah	Obadiah	Obadiah
		Death of Obadiah
Jonah	Chapters of Jonah	Chapters of Jonah
Death of Jonah	Jonah	Jonah
		Death of Jonah
Nahum	Chapters of Nahum	Chapters of Nahum
Death of Nahum	Nahum	Nahum
		Death of Nahum
Habakkuk	Chapters of Habakkuk	Chapters of Habakkuk
Death of Habakkuk	Habakkuk	Habakkuk
		Death of Habakkuk
Zephaniah	Chapters of Zephaniah	Chapters of Zephaniah
Death of Zephaniah	Zephaniah	Zephaniah
		Death of Zephaniah
Haggai	Preface to Haggai	Chapters of Haggai
Death of Haggai	Haggai	Haggai
		Death of Haggai
Zechariah	Chapters of Zechariah	Chapters of Zechariah
Death of Zechariah	Zechariah	Zechariah
		Death of Zechariah
Malachi	Chapters of Malachi	Chapters of Malachi
Death of Malachi	Malachi	Malachi
		Death of Malachi
	Death of the Twelve Prophets	
	Death of Daniel	
	Preface to Jeremiah	Preface to Jeremiah
	Chapters of Jermeiah	Chapters of Jeremiah
	Jeremiah	Jeremiah
	Baruch	Baruch
	Lamentations	Lamentations
	Prayer of Jeremiah	
	Death of Jeremiah	
	Preface to Daniel	Preface to Daniel
	Chapter of Daniel	Chapters to Daniel
	Daniel	Daniel
		Death of Daniel
Psalms		
Proverbs		
Ecclesiasticus		

Erznka, 1269	Cilicia, 1319	Baberdatsi, Lvov, 1619
Song of Songs		
Wisdom		
Daniel		
Judith		
Ezekiel		
Esther		
Tobit		
	Preface to Ezekiel	Preface to Ezekiel
	Chapters of Ezekiel	Chapters of Ezekiel
	Ezekiel	Ezekiel
	Death of Ezekiel	
Chapters of Matthew		
Chapters of Mark		
Chapters of Luke		
Letter of Eusebius	Letter of Eusebius	Letter of Eusebius
Canon Tables 1–10	Canon Tables	Canon Tables 1–10
	Chapters of Matthew	Chapters of Matthew
	Synoptics of the Gospels	Synoptics of the Gospels
	Preface to Matthew	Preface to Matthew
Matthew	Matthew	Matthew
	Chapters of Mark	Chapters of Mark
	Preface to Mark	Preface to Mark
Mark	Mark	Mark
	Chapters of Luke	Chapters of Luke
	Preface to Luke	Preface to Luke
Luke	Luke	Luke
	Chapters of John	Chapters of John
	Preface to John	Preface to John
John	John	John
Commentary on Revelation		
Chapters of Revelation		
Revelation		
Repose of St John		
Preface to Paul		
Testimonies of Paul		
Chapters of Romans		
Romans		
Chapters of I Corinthians		
I Corinthians		
Chapters of II Corinthians		
II Corinthians		
Chapters of Galatians		
Galatians		
Chapters of Ephesians		
Ephesians		
Chapters of Philippians		
Philippians		
Chapters of Colossians		
Colossians		
Chapters of Thessalonians		
I Thessalonians		
Chapters of II Thessalonians		
II Thessalonians		
Chapters of Hebrews		
Hebrews		

Erznka, 1269	Cilicia, 1319	Baberdatsi, Lvov, 1619
Chapters of I Timothy		
I Timothy		
Chapters of II Timothy		
II Timothy		
Chapters of Titus		
Titus		
Chapters to Philipians		
Philippians		
Colophon of Euthalius		
Testimony		
Sea voyage of Paul		
Preface to Acts	Preface to Acts	Preface to Acts
	Headings of Acts	Headings of Acts
Chapters of Acts	Chapters of Acts	Chapters of Acts
Acts of the Apostles	Acts of the Apostles	Acts of the Apostles
Preface to the Seven Epistles	Preface to the Catholic epistles	Preface to the Seven Epistles
Headings of the Epistles		
	Preface to James	
	Chapters of James	Chapters of James
James	James	James
	Preface to I Peter	
Chapters of I Peter	Chapters of I Peter	Chapters of Peter
I Peter	I Peter	I Peter
	Preface to II Peter	
Chapters of II Peter	Chapters of II Peter	Chapters of II Peter
II Peter	II Peter	II Peter
	Preface to I John	
Chapters of I John	Chapters of I John	Chapters of I John
I John	I John	I John
	Preface to II John	
Chapters of II John	Chapters of II John	Chapters of II John
II John	II John	II John
	Preface to III John	
Chapters of III John	Chapters of III John	Chapters of III John
III John	III John	III John
	Preface to Jude	
Chapters of Jude	Chapters of Jude	Chapters of Jude
Jude	Jude	Jude
Epistle of Euthalius	Epistle of Euthalius	Epistle of Euthalius
	Preface to Revelation	
	Chapters of Revelation	
	Revelation	
	Preface to Paul	Preface to Paul
	Testimonies of Paul	Testimonies of Paul
	Contents of lections	Contents of Paul
	Preface	
	Preface to Romans	
	Chapters of Romans	Chapters of Romans
	Romans	Romans
	Preface to I Corinthians	
	Chapters of I Corinthians	Chapters of I Corinthians
	I Corinthians	I Corinthians
	Preface to II Corinthians	
	Chapters of II Corinthians	Chapters of II Corinthians
	II Corinthians	II Corinthians

Erznka, 1269	Cilicia, 1319	Baberdatsi, Lvov, 1619
		Letter of the Corinthians
		III Corinthians
	Preface to Galatians	
	Chapters of Galatians	Chapters of Galatians
	Galatians	Galatians
	Preface to Ephesians	Chapters of Ephesians
	Chapters of Ephesians	Ephesians
	Ephesians	
	Preface to Philippians	Chapters of Philippians
	Chapters of Philippians	
	Philippians	Philippians
	Preface to Colossians	
	Chapters of Colossians	Chapters of Colossians
	Colossians	Colossians
	Preface to I Thessalonians	
	Chapters of I Thessalonians	Chapters of I Thessalonians
	I Thessalonians	I Thessalonians
	Preface to II Thessalonians	
	Chapters of II Thessalonians	Chapters of II Thessalonians
	II Thessalonians	II Thessalonians
	Preface to Hebrews	
	Chapters of Hebrews	Chapters of Hebrews
	Hebrews	Hebrews
	Preface to I Timothy	
	Chapters of I Timothy	Chapters of I Timothy
	I Timothy	I Timothy
	Preface to II Timothy	
	Chapters of II Timothy	Chapters of II Timothy
	II Timothy	II Timothy
	Preface to Titus	
	Chapters of Titus	Chapters of Titus
	Titus	Titus
	Preface to Philemon	
	Chapters of Philemon	Chapters of Philemon
	Philemon	Philemon
	Colophon of Euthalius	Colophon of Euthalius
	Preface to Euthalius	Preface to Euthalius
	Sea Voyage of Paul	
	Letter of the Corinthians	
	III Corinthians	
		Preface to Revelation
		Chapters of Revelation
		Revelation
		Repose of John
		Poem by Ghazar
		List of Armenian verses
		List according to Latin Vulgate

Bibliography

Primary sources

Aṙak'el Siwnetsi, *Adamagirk'* [*Adambook*] ed. A. Madoyan. Erevan, 1989.

Bede, *A history of the English Church and People*, transl. by E. Shirley Price. Harmondsworth, 1955.

Eghishē, *Vasn Vardanats ew Hayots Paterazmin* [*History of Vardan and the Armenian war*], ed. E.Ter Minasyan. English transl. by Robert W. Thomson, 1982.

Ephrem, the Syrian, *Srboyn Ep'remi matenagrut'iwnk'* [*The collected works of St Ephrem in Armenian translation, comprising the commentaries on Genesis, Exodus, Leviticus, Numbers, Deuteronomy, Joshua, Judges, Kings, and Chronicles* (vol.1); *Commentary on the Diatessaron, transl. of the Gospels and Homilies* (II); *Commentary on the 14 Epistless of St Paul (III); Homilies and Prayers* (IV). Venice, 1836.

Ephrem, the Syrian, 'The Commentary of Ephrem on Acts', tr, Conybeare, F.C., in *The Beginnings of Christianity*, eds. Jackson, F. and Lake, K., London, 1926.

Ephrem, the Syrian, 'Commentaire de l'Evangile Concordant, Version armenienne', ed. Leloir, L., *Corpus Scriptorum Christianurum Orientalium*, 137 (Latin), 145 (Arm), Louvain, 1954–55.

Ghazar P'arpetsi, *Patmut'iwn Hayots* [*History of the Armenians*], ed. G.Ter–Mkrtchian & St. Malkhasian. Tiflis, 1904. English transl. by Robert W.Thomson, 1991.

Gregory of Narek, *The Lamentations, Mystic soliquies with God*, transl. and ed. By Mischa Kudian. London, 1977.

Grigor Tat'evatsi, *Meknut'iwn Saghmosats* [*Commentary on the Psalms*], comp. by Armine K'yoshkeryan. Erevan, 1993.

Grigor Pahlawuni Magistros, *Taghasatsut'iwnk' Grigori Magistrosi Pahlawunwoy* [*The poetry of*]. Venice, 1868.

Hamam Areweltsi, *Meknut'iwn Aṙakats* [*Commentary on the Proverbs*], compl. Mkhit'ar Khn. Saribekyan. Erevan, 1994.

Khatchikyan, Levon, *Eghisei 'Araradsots meknut'iwně* [*Commentary on Genesis*], ed. by Levon Ter Petrosyan. Erevan, 1992.

Koriwn, *Vark' Mashtotsi* [*Life of Mashtots*], ed. M.Abeghian. English transl. by Bedros Norehad. U.S.A., 1964.

Movses Khorenatsi, *Patmut'iwn Hayots* [*History of the Armenians*] ed. M.Abeghian & S.Yarut'iwnian. Erevan, 1991. English transl. by Robert W.Thomson, Cambridge, Mass., 1978.

Nerses Shnorhali, *Yisus Ordi* [*Jesus the Son*] ed. Avet Set'ian. Madras, 1792.

P'awstos Buzand, *Patmut'iwn Hayots* [*The Epic Histories*] ed. St. Malkhasian. Erevan, 1947. English transl. By Nina G.Garsoian, Cambridge, Mass., 1989.

Sargis Shnorhali, *Meknut'iwn eot'ants t'ght'ots Kat'oghikeayts* [*Commentary on the seven catholic epistles*]. Constantinople, 1828; reprinted Jerusalem, 1998.

Step'anos Siwnetsi, *Meknut'iwn tchorits Awetarantchats* [*Commentary on the Four Gospels*], comp. by Garegin Yovsepian. Athens, 1988; reprinted in Erevan, 1994.

Step'anos Taronatsi (Asoghik) *Patmutiwn Tiezerakan* [*Universal History*] ed. St.Malkhasian. St.Petersburg, 1885.

T'ovmay Ardsruni, *Patmut'iwn tann Ardsruneats* [*History of the House of the Ardsruni*]. Constantinople, 1852. English transl. by Robert W. Thomson. Detroit 1985.

Secondary sources

Abrahamyan, A.G., *Hay gir ev grtchut'yan patmut'yun* [*History of Armenian script and paleography*]. Erevan, 1959.

Ackroyd, P.R. & Evans, C.F., *The Cambridge history of the Bible*.Vol. I: From the beginnings to Jerome. II: The West from the Fathers to the Reformation.Cambridge, 1987.

Aghbalian, N., *Patmut'iwn hay grakanut'ean* [*History of Armenian literature*]. Beyrouth, 1947

Ajamian, Shahe, 'Oskanean Astuadsatchuntchi kanonĕ' [The canon of the Oskanian Bible], *Sion* 2–3(1966), 72–77; 4(1966), 205–207; 8(1966), 413–414.

Ajamian, Shahe, *Tutsak Astuadsashuntch mateani hayeren dzeragirnerun* = Grand catalogue des manuscrits Arméniens de la Bible. Lisbonne, 1992.

Ajamian, S. & M.E. Stone, eds. *Text and context. Studies in the Armenian New Testament*. Atlanta, Georgia, 1994.

Anasyan, H.S. Hay *Hamabarbarayin grakanut'yunĕ ev Hay matenagrut'yan hamabarbarĕ* [*Armenian concordance literature and the concordance of Armenian literature*]. Ějmiadsin, 1972.

Anasyan, *H.S., Astuadsatchuntch mateani haykakan bnagirĕ* = *Bibliae Sacrae Versio Armena* (Bibliographia) Erevan, 1976.

Bedekian, A.A., *Patmakan aknark Astuadsatchuntchi t'argmanut'eants vray* [A brief history of the printing of the Modern Armenian Bible]. New York, 1953.

Bedekian A.A., *The golden age in the fifth century. An introduction to Armenian literature in perspective*. New York, 1963.

Bidwell, John, *A thousand years of the Bible. An exhibition of manuscripts from the J.Paul Getty Museum Malibu*. Los Angeles, 1991.

Brock, Sebastian P., *The Bible in the Syriac tradition*. India, 1989.

Bruce, F.F., *The Books and the Parchments. Some chapters on the transmission of the Bible*. London, 1953.

Burchard, Christoph ed. *Armenia and the Bible. Papers presented to the International Symposium held at Heidelberg July 16–19, 1990*. Atlanta, Georgia, 1993.

Canton, William, *A history of the British & Foreign Bible Society*. London, 1904.

Casey, R.P., 'The Armenian Marcionites and the Diatessaron', *Journal of Biblical Literature LVII* (1938), 185–194.

Colwell, E., 'Mark 16:9–20 in the Armenian version', *Journal of Biblical Literature 56* (1937), 369–386.

Conybeare, F.C., 'Armenian version of the OT' & 'Armenian version of NT' in *A Dictionary of the Bible*, ed. by James Hastings.London, 1906.

Conybeare, F.C., 'An Armenian Diatessaron', *The Journal of Theological Studies XXV* (1924), 232–245.

Cox, Claude, E., 'Biblical studies and the Armenian Bible, 1955–1980' , *Revue Biblique* I (Janvier,1982), 99–13.

Darlow, T.H., & H.F. Moule, *Historical catalogue of the printed editions of Holy Scripture in the library of the British & Foreign Bible Society.* Vol.II. Polyglotts and languages other than English. London, 1911.

Ferahian, S., 'S.Grots Hayk. t'argmanut'ean skhalnerun ew arawelut'eants nmuysh mě' [The errors and advantages of the Armenian translation of the Bible], *Bazmavep* (1935), 419–424.

Ghazaryan, Vigen, 'Kerparvestn ěst Nerses Shnorhalu'[The theory of art according to Nerses Shnorhali] *Lraber Hasarakakan Git.* I (1975), 68– 75.

Ghazaryan, Vigen, 'The doctrine of colour in commentaries on canon tables', *Atti V Simposio Internazionale di Arte Armena* (Venice, 1991), 687–694.

Ghazaryan, Vigen, *Khoranneri meknut'yunner = Commentaries on the Canon Tables.* Erevan, 1995.

Goodspeed, Edgar J., A *history of early Christian literature.* Revised and enlarged by R.M. Grant. Chicago, 1966.

Hayrapetian, S.P., *Hayots hin ev mijnadarean grakanut'ean patmut'iwn* [*History of ancient and medieval Armenian literature*]. Erevan, 1994.

Johnson, Bo, 'Some remarks on the marginal notes in Armenian I Samuel', *Armenian and Biblical Studies,* M.E. Stone, ed. Jerusalem, 1976.

Kenyon, Frederic, *Our Bible and the ancient manuscripts.* London, 1948.

Khatchikyan, L.S., *XV dari hayeren dzeragreri hishtakaranner* [*Colophons of XVth century Armenian manuscripts.I* (1401–1450); II (1451–1480)]. Erevan, 1955; 1958.

Khatchikyan, L.S., *XIV dari hayeren dzeragreri hishatakaranner* [*Colophons of XIVth century manuscripts*]. Erevan, 1950.

Khatchikyan, L.S.ed. *Banber Matenadarani 7* (1964), [dedicated to the 1600th Birthday anniversary of Mesrop Mashtots].

Kiwlesěrian, Babgen, *Hayastaneayts ekeghetsin hingerord daru mej* [*The Armenian church in the fifth century*]. Constantinople, 1912.

Klijn, A.F., 'An old witness of the Armenian text', *Journal of Theological Studies II* (October, 1951), 168–170.

Lawrence, Edward A., *Modern Missions in the East. Their Methods, Successes, and limitations,* New York, 1895.

Leloir, Louis, Saint Ephrem. Commentaire de l'evangile concordant. *CSCO* 137, Scriptores armeniaci 1: Armenian text; *CSCO* 145, Scriptores armeniaci 2; Latin translation. Louvain, 1953–54.

Lockwood, Wilfrid, *The Word of God. Biblical manuscripts at the Chester Beatty Library, Dublin.* Dublin, 1987.

Mango, Cyril, *The art of the Byzantine Empire 312–1453.* London, 1986.

Mathews, Thomas F., and Roger S. Wieck, *Treasures in Heaven. Armenian illuminated manuscripts.* Princeton University Press, 1994.

Mathews, Thomas F., & Avedis K. Sanjian, *Armenian Gospel iconography. The tradition of the Glajor Gospel.* Washington D.C., 1991.

Merk, August, 'Die Armenischen Evanglien und ihre Vorlage' *Biblica, vii* (1926), 40–70.

Metzger, Bruce, M., *The early versions of the New Testament. Their origin, transmission and limitations.* Oxford, 1977.

Metzger, Bruce, M., *The text of the New Testament. Its transmission, corruption and restoration. 2nd ed.* Oxford, 1985.

Murad, Frederik', *Yaytnut'eann Yovhannu hin hay t'argmanut'iwn* [*The early Armnian translation of the Revelation of John*]. Jerusalem, 1905–1911.

Nersessian, Vrej, *Catalogue of early Armenian books 1512–1850.* London, 1980

Nersessian, Vrej, 'Armenian manuscripts of the Holy Scriptures' in *Historical catalogue of the manuscripts of Bible House Library*, compiled by M. Rosaria Falivene and edited by Alan F.Jesson. Bible Society, 1982, 28–32.

Nersessian, Vrej, *Armenian illuminated Gospel Books.* London, 1987.

Nersessian, Vrej, 'Bible in Armenian translation', in *The Everyman Companion to East European literature*, ed. by R.B. Pynsent. London, 1993; reprinted in *Reader's Encyclopedia of Eastern European Literature.* London, 1993.

Nersessian, Vrej, *A bibliography of articles on Armenian studies in western journals*, 1869–1995. London, 1997.

Nersoyan, Tiran, *Divine Liturgy of the Armenian Apostolic Orthodox Church with Variables, complete rubrics and Commentary.* Fifth edition by V.N. Nersessian. London, 1984.

Nersoyan, Tiran, 'The Bible in the Armenian Church', in *Armenian Church Historical Studies*, ed. V.N. Nersessian. New York, 1996.

Pattie, T.S., *Manuscripts of the Bible.Greek Bibles in the British Library.* Revised edition. London, 1979.

Petrosyan, Eznik, 'Avetaranneri miǰnadaryan Haykakan meknut'yunner' [Medieval Armenian commentaries on the Gospels], *Ēǰmiadsin* 1 (1982), 35–41.

Petrosyan, Levon, 'Saghmosneri hayeren t'argmanut'yunĕ', [The Armenian translation of Pslams], *Ēǰmiadsin* 6&9 (1975), 8–9 (1976).

Pogharian, Norayr, 'Sirak'ay hin hay t'argmanut'iwnnerĕ' [Early Armenian translations of the Book of Sirach], *Sion* 5 (1936), 150–153.

Pogharian, Norayr, 'Mnatsordats girk'erun hin hay t'argmanut'iwnnerĕ' [Early Armenian translations of the Chronicles], *Sion* 4 (1937), 109–114.

Pogharian, Norayr, 'Partawi zhoghovin kanonnerun verǰin yoduadsĕ' [The last clause of the canons of the Council of Partav], *Sion* 1–3 (1944), 26–27.

Pogharian, Norayr, 'Astuadsatchuntchi hayeren hin t'argmanut'iwnnerĕ' [The early Armenian translations of the Bible], *Sion* 3–4 (1945), 47–50, 107–112; 145–149.

Pogharian, Norayr, 'Oskanean Astuadsashuntchĕ S.Grots kanoni hayetsaketen' [The Oskanian Bible from the perspective of the Armenian canon], *Sion* 2–3 (1966), 70–71.

Pogharian, Norayr, *Hay groghner* [*Armenian writers V–XVIIth centuries*]. Jerusalem, 1971.

Sanjian, Avedis K., *Colophons of Armenian manuscripts 1301–1480.* Cambridge, Mass., 1969.

Sanjian, Avedis K., 'Esayi Ntchetsi and Biblical exegesis' in *Armenia and the Bible*, ed. C. Burchard, 1993, 185–193.

Shamlian, Daniel, 'Surb Grots kanonakan ew Erkrordakanon girk'erĕ' [The canonical and uncanonical books of the Bible], *Sion* 2–3 (1966), 83–87.

Shamlian, Daniel, 'Yovhannu Yaytnut'ean girk'' [John's Book of Revelations], *Sion* 7 (1966), 348–353.

Stone, M.E., *Selected studies in Pseudepigrapha and Apocrypha, with special reference to the Armenian tradition.* Leiden, 1991.

Tēr Minasyan, E. 'Neue Peschittahandschriften.I.Aram

Datians syrische Pesitta–Handschrift des Neuen Testaments in Etschmiadsin', *ZNW* (Berlin 1905), 282–284.

Tēr Minasyan, E., *Oskedari Hay grakanut'yunĕ* [The Armenian literature of the 'golden age']. Erevan, 1946

Terian, Abraham, 'The Bible in verse by Gregory Magistros', in *Armenia and the Bible*, ed. C. Burchard, 1993, 213–219.

Teryan, Vahan, 'Astvadsashntchi askharhabar t'argmanut'yan ev hratatakut'yan patmut'yunits' [Brief history the modern Armenian translations and printings of the Armenian Bible], *Ējmiadsin* 11–12 (1966), 176 189. Note. The whole issue is dedicated to 300th anniversary of the printing of the Oskanian Bible, see also *Hask 3–5* (1966), *Sion* 2–3 (1966).

Thomson, Robert W., 'Aspects of Medieval Armenian Exegesis' in *New Perspectives to Medieval Armenian Language and Literature*, ed. J.J.S. Weitenberg. Atlanta, GA., 1995, 47–61.

Yushardzan Astuadsashuntchi Hayeren t'argmanut'ean 1500– ameaki [*Monument to the 1500th hundred anniversary of the translation of the Armenian Bible*]. Jerusalem,1938.

Yusik' *episkopos*, 'Britanakan Astuadsashntchi Surb grots hayeren t'argmanut'iwnnerĕ' [The Armenian translations of the Bible by the British Bible Society], *Ararat* (1885), 435–439.

Weitzmann, Kurt, 'The narrative and liturgical Gospel illustrations', in *Studies in Classical & Byzantine manuscript illumination*, edited by Herbert L. Kessler. Chicago, 1971, 247–270.

Zekiyan, Levon, 'Eghishē as witness of the ecclesiology of the early Armenian Church', in *East of Byzantium: Syria and Armenia in the formative period*. Dumbarton Oakes, 1982, 187–19

Index